SYDNEY PRECINCTS

A curated guide to the city's best shops, eateries, bars and other hangouts

SYDNEY PRECINCTS

A curated guide to the city's best shops, eateries, bars and other hangouts

CHRIS CARROLL

hardie grant publishing

CONTENTS

WELCOME

Welcome to *Sydney Precincts*; a guide to the best venues this glorious city has to offer. Broken into 19 precincts, this book will give you an insider look into some of Sydney's best suburbs and what makes them so stellar.

Think of this book as a collection of amazing, intriguing, sometimes unexpected, but jaw-droppingly awesome places to eat, drink, shop and play. The hardest part about authoring this book was having a limited number of pages to try and squeeze in all of the venues I wanted to include!

Sydney is like no other city in the world. Its harbour is breathtaking at every turn and its stunning natural beauty, Harbour Bridge, headlands, yachts, marinas, and surf beaches make it cosmopolitan with a view.

In each precinct I've also interviewed a local who knows their suburb inside out. They reveal their fave places to hang out, so that you know where the locals go.

The suburbs of Sydney are like an extended family; they're all intertwined and uniquely different. Diversity is king here. The kind of day you'll have at Bondi Beach is world's apart from the day you'll have in Newtown. As you travel you'll come to find the precinct that you feel most at home in.

You might even, as I have, hold a love for several pockets and for different reasons. I've lived and worked in almost all of these precincts and if there's one thing I've learnt, it's that no suburb has it all. And I kinda like it that way.

Getting around doesn't have to be confusing, and in most cases public transport is your best bet, with ferries being both a transport means and a spectacular way to sightsee.

And if you get stuck, ask a local. Sydneysiders (for the most part) are on the ball when it comes to getting around. They've experienced all the different modes of public transport, they can tell you when you're better off walking rather than waiting in traffic, and they know great places to stop for a coffee (we do a pretty good brew no matter what our Melbourne rivals might say!).

It's time to discover the best experiences Sydney has to offer. Enjoy!

Chris Carroll

GLADESVILLE

HUNTLEYS COVE

HUNTLEYS POINT

HENLEY

ABBOTSFORD

CHISWICK

DRUMMOYNE

WAREEMBA

RUSSELL LEA

FIVE DOCK

RODD POINT

HABERFIELD

ASHFIELD

SUMMER HILL

LEWISHAM

PETERSHAM

DULWICH HILL

EARLWOOD

TURRELLA

WOLLI CREEK

HUNTERS HILL

LONGUEVILLE

GREENWICH

WOOLLOONECRAFT

NORTH SYDNEY

NEUTRA BAY

WOOLWICH

WAVERTON

LAVENDER BAY

KURRA POI

BIRCHGROVE

MCMAHONS POINT

MILSONS POINT

KIRRIBILLI

BALMAIN

BALMAIN EAST

SYDNEY HARBOUR, CIRCULAR QUAY AND THE ROCKS
218

BALMAIN AND ROZELLE
10

ROZELLE

BARANGAROO

THE ROCKS

LILYFIELD

PYRMONT

PYRMONT AND HAYMARKET
158

SYDNEY CBD
206

SYDNEY

POTTS POIN

GLEBE, ANNANDALE AND LEICHHARDT
98

POTTS POINT TO WOOLLOOMOOLOO
146

LEICHHARDT

FOREST LODGE

GLEBE

ULTIMO

HAYMARKET

DARLINGHURST

ANNANDALE

CAMPERDOWN

CHIPPENDALE

DARLINGHURST AND PADDINGTON
60

PADDINGTO

STANMORE

DARLINGTON

DARLINGTON

SURRY HILLS
192

NEWTOWN

REDFERN AND WATERLOO
170

SURRY HILLS

NEWTOWN AND ERSKINEVILLE
122

EVELEIGH

REDFERN

MOORE PARK

ENMORE

ENMORE, MARRICKVILLE AND ST PETERS
86

ERSKINEVILLE

WATERLOO

ALEXANDRIA

ZETLAND

MARRICKVILLE

BEACONSFIELD

ST PETERS

ALEXANDRIA AND ROSEBERY
XVI

KENSINGTON

SYDENHAM

TEMPE

MASCOT

ROSEBERY

KINGSFORD

EASTLAKES

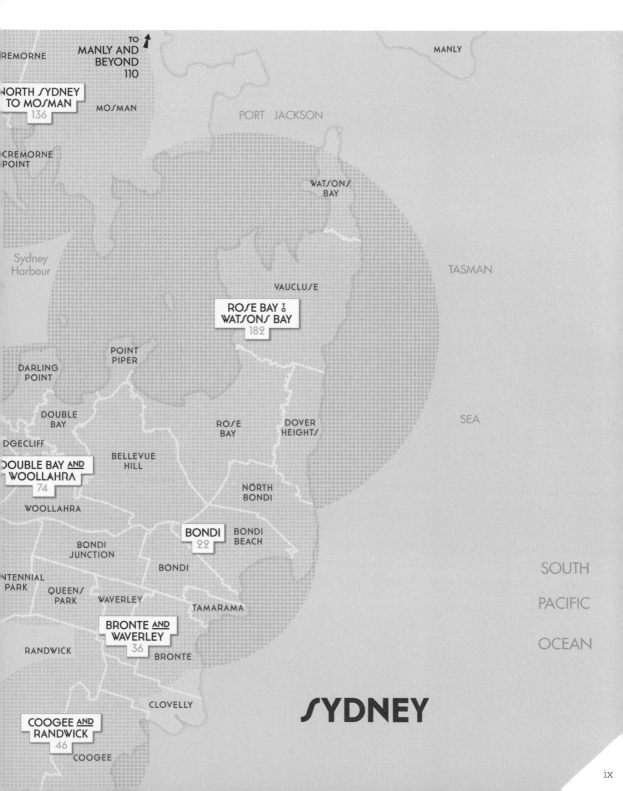

CREMORNE

TO
MANLY AND
BEYOND
110

MANLY

**NORTH SYDNEY
TO MOSMAN**
136

MOSMAN

PORT JACKSON

CREMORNE
POINT

WATSONS
BAY

Sydney
Harbour

TASMAN

VAUCLUSE

**ROSE BAY TO
WATSONS BAY**
182

POINT
PIPER

DARLING
POINT

SEA

DOUBLE
BAY

ROSE
BAY

DOVER
HEIGHTS

DGECLIFF

BELLEVUE
HILL

**DOUBLE BAY AND
WOOLLAHRA**
74

WOOLLAHRA

NORTH
BONDI

BONDI
22

BONDI
BEACH

BONDI
JUNCTION

BONDI

NTENNIAL
PARK

QUEENS
PARK

WAVERLEY

TAMARAMA

SOUTH

**BRONTE AND
WAVERLEY**
36

PACIFIC

RANDWICK

BRONTE

OCEAN

CLOVELLY

SYDNEY

**COOGEE AND
RANDWICK**
46

COOGEE

For me, a fabulous Sydney day starts with brunch. But those of you who are into a far earlier rise will want to experience a killer breakfast. If there's one place to do that it's at the beach. **SHUK** (*see* page 027) in Bondi is a good spot to start, followed by a walk along the iconic beach to see the famous lifesavers and surfers. Everyone around Bondi Beach will be exercising early, so sit on the sand of a morning and take in the scenery.

If you want to save your seaside adventure for later in the day, swing by **Indigo** in Double Bay (*see* page 082) and grab breakfast there. It's just as relaxed and there are some great retail outlets nearby if you want to pick up a pair of shoes.

I'm addicted to home decor, so on a weekend morning you'll find me popping my head into places like **Koskela** in Rosebery (*see* page 002). While you're in that area, you have to go try the cakes on offer at **Black Star Pastry** (*see* page 004). They really cannot be beaten.

If you're into a faster-paced shopping experience and you've got your heart set on fashion finds, get the train to Town Hall and explore the **QVB** and **Galleries Victoria**. Not only are these buildings historic and artistic, but the shopping is just as worth a view. Hop over to nearby **Strand Arcade** (*see* page 208) for some amazing designer fashion moments.

Lunch, especially if it's sunny outside, calls for a trip to the harbour. You can't go past either fish and chips on the rooftop at **The Glenmore Hotel** at The Rocks (*see* page 225), or a few drinks and nibbles at **Opera Bar** at Sydney Opera House (*see* page 224), which is a truly lavish experience right on the waterfront (and they do some tasty pizzas).

Wherever I've lived, I always found a good spot to run, which has enabled me to discover the local picnic spots. **Centennial Park** is so mammoth you'll be spoilt for

choice in terms of where you lay down your picnic blanket. **Sydney Park** has also come leaps and bounds over the years and is a dog-lover's paradise. On your way to Sydney Park, grab some picnic fare from nearby **Salt Meats Cheese** (*see* page 007). Or do the **Botanic Gardens** in the city and have an afternoon wine at **Andrew Boy Charlton Pool**.

If you're after an afternoon of culture, head to the **Museum of Contemporary Art** (MCA, *see* page 220) at The Rocks, or visit some of the other popular art galleries around the city (*see* page xii).

An afternoon ferry trip to Manly or Rose Bay is the best way to admire the stunning harbour, Harbour Bridge, yachts and waterfront properties. Go a little further and have a bite to eat at **The Boathouse at Palm Beach** (*see* page 116), or dig into something more substantial at **Papi Chulo** (*see* page 115).

For dinner, set your compass for either Surry Hills or Newtown. Surry Hills is easy to get to from the CBD and has many reliable haunts, like **The Winery** (*see* page 203) for a drink and **The Nepalese Kitchen** (*see* page 200) for a feed. In Newtown, **Earl's Juke Joint** (*see* page 129) is the place to go for a cocktail, though **Corridor** (*see* page 132) also puts on roaring times and has dinner options to boot!

The Inner West is full of amazing night spots, such as **The Different Drummer** (*see* page 106) and **The Little Guy** (*see* page 106), both in Glebe, which is one of the few areas with no lockout laws (which means you can pub crawl or bar hop with ease).

Sydney is sure to put on a good show! It's all big lights and loads of razzle dazzle (especially of an evening), but underpinning that is a laid-back beach culture with a lot of history waiting to be uncovered. You just have to look for it.

CENTRAL SYDNEY

Sydney Opera House
This modernist masterpiece has a fascinating story behind it – go on a guided tour to discover the inside story.

Sydney Harbour Bridge
Walk across the bridge from The Rocks to Kirribilli for the best view in Sydney. Look away if you're scared of heights – you can also walk to the top with a BridgeClimb.

GALLERIES AND MUSEUMS

Art Gallery of New South Wales (AGNSW)
Housed in a stately old building, the gallery is famous for both its permanent collection and exhibitions. Come for Art After Hours if you can!

Museum of Contemporary Art
The MCA has recently had a major upgrade, and now features a boxy contemporary extension adjoining the original 1953 building.

Australian National Maritime Museum
The Maritime Museum is a nautical playground, with ships including old naval vessels and a replica of Cook's *Endeavour* moored next to the museum ready to be boarded.

Susannah Place Museum
The four terraces that house the Susannah Place Museum were built in 1844 and are some of the oldest in town. They are a remarkable glimpse into early life in Sydney.

ARTS, HISTORY & SPORTS

Royal Botanic Gardens and Government House
The Royal Botanic Gardens spans the harbour from the Sydney Opera House to the AGNSW and enfolds Government House. Don't miss the view from Lady Macquarie's Chair.

Andrew Boy Charlton Pool
Boy, what a view! The pool is just down from AGNSW and overlooks Garden Island. Have an afternoon aperitif at the cafe.

Macquarie Street (Hyde Park Barracks, The Mint, State Library)
This is Sydney's power street, featuring Parliament House and offices of the rich and the influential. It also has some historical buildings, like Hyde Park Barracks (convict history done for kids), The Mint and the State Library of New South Wales (which often has great exhibitions). Sydney Museum is just off Macquarie Street.

Queen Victoria Building (QVB)
It's a shopping centre, but not like you're used to. The building was built in the late 19th century, and has all the flourishes and fancies of the era.

Sydney Theatre Company (The Wharf)
Sydney's premier theatre company has its home at Hickson Bay. Even if you don't see a show (although it's highly recommended), have a drink at The Theatre Bar at the End of the Wharf and watch the sun set over Sydney.

Powerhouse Museum

One of Sydney's most interesting museums, Powerhouse Museum focuses on innovation, science and design with interactive exhibits, including a replica space shuttle.

The University of Sydney

The University of Sydney's grand old sandstone quadrangle houses museums, including the Nicholson Museum, which has a remarkable collection of antiquities.

Carriageworks

An innovative arts space built into the old Eveleigh Rail Yards, Carriageworks has an exciting program of events, plus a cafe and a farmers' market of a Saturday you can really sink your teeth into.

Brett Whiteley studio

Managed by AGNSW, this was the working studio of one of Sydney's most prominent artists, Brett Whiteley. It's open on Fridays, Saturdays and Sundays.

FURTHER EXPLORATION

Cockatoo Island

Cockatoo Island looks like a ghost island, its rocky escarpments home to ruins and abandoned factories ... Catch a ferry out and explore or visit one of the art festivals held on the island.

Fort Denison

This tiny fort is just off Garden Island and was built to defend the harbour from attacks. Come for lunch.

Sydney Tower Eye and SKYWALK

You can walk around an external glass balcony at the top of the tallest building in Sydney – don't worry, you'll get a harness!

OUTER WEST

Old Government House

One of the oldest buildings in Sydney, this charming holiday house for early governors is in Parramatta Park.

Newington Armory and Playground

An old naval area that used to store, well, armaments, you can explore the area by bike and have lunch at the cafe, and sneak in a play on the adventure playground.

SYDNEY ATTRACTIONS

NORTH SHORE

Ferry to Manly
There's no better way to get to Manly. The ferry from Circular Quay takes you past Sydney's most exclusive suburbs and North and South Head. More than half the fun is getting there!

Taronga Zoo
On Bradleys Head overlooking the harbour, the giraffes at Taronga have the best view in town.

Wendy's Secret Garden
This secret garden was built by Wendy Whiteley, wife of famous artist Brett Whiteley, around old rail tracks in Lavender Bay.

Luna Park
At Milsons Point just under the Harbour Bridge, Luna Park has classic amusement park rides. It's right next to North Sydney Olympic Pool.

Barrenjoey Lighthouse
You can hike up to this historic lighthouse overlooking Palm Beach and Pittwater, with views up to the Central Coast. The lighthouse is part of Ku-ring-gai Chase National Park, which also has notable Aboriginal sites.

Manly to Spit Bridge walk
Starting at the Spit Bridge, this 10km walk weaves and winds around Middle Harbour all the way to Manly Beach.

EASTERN SUBURBS

Elizabeth Bay House
With an expansive view over the harbour, this colonial mansion tells a rags to riches to rags tale – with a view, naturally.

Horby Lighthouse
A short walk from Watsons Bay, this lighthouse marks the edge of South Head. Watch out (or not) for the nudist beach and old armaments on the way.

Bondi to Coogee Walk
Sydney's most famous walk, this cliff-top walk starts at Bondi, dips in and out of Tamarama Beach, Bronte Beach, Waverley Cemetery, and ends at Coogee. Sculpture by the Sea happens along the walk October to November.

Centennial Park
This grand Victorian park was inaugurated in 1888, and features expansive gardens and avenues, perfect for horse-riding.

Nielson Park
An inner harbour beach near Vaucluse House, Nielson Park has a shark net and an old world kiosk. Follow the walking trail along the cliffs to Strickland House and Milk Beach.

FURTHER OUT

Royal National Park
Blue Mountains (Katoomba, Leura and the Three Sisters)
Jenolan Caves
Windsor

AIRPORT

Sydney Airport, home to both the international and domestic airports, is just outside of the city centre – you might fly in over the Sydney Harbour Bridge if you're lucky!

The easiest way to get into the city from the airport is by train, and there are stations at both the domestic and international airports. You can buy a ticket at the station.

A one-way adult ticket to the central business district (CBD) is $17; definitely your cheapest option unless you can convince someone to pick you up. Trains leave approximately every 10 minutes and it takes around 13 minutes to get to Central Station, Sydney's biggest transport hub. From Central you can get a bus or train to most areas of the metropolis. If you'd prefer a taxi, taxis are available at the designated taxi rank and a trip into the CBD will cost around $50.

PUBLIC TRANSPORT

Sydney is a bus town, and the network connects all areas of the city to the CBD. Most buses will stop at Central, but it's always a good idea to check the timetable online. You can also catch trains to many areas of Sydney and the network is currently being upgraded to reach more parts of the city. Ferries are the easiest way to connect to harbour suburbs like Watsons Bay (*see* page 182) and Manly (*see* page 110). Sydney's light rail will soon extend through the city, so expect disruptions while this is being built.

The easiest way to get around is to get an Opal card. You can get a free Opal card from the Central Station Transport Customer Service Centre. The Opal card can be used across Sydney's public transport network; top up at the customer service centre or at a 7/Eleven store.

DINING OUT

Eating and drinking is a sport in Sydney – one the locals excel at! If you want to dine at any of Sydney's top restaurants, you'll need to book at least a few weeks in advance.

Tipping in Sydney is entirely at the diner's discretion, but it is expected at fine-dining restaurants, where the service will be particularly top notch. Hardly anyone tips at bars or cafes, but if you have a few spare coins, the staff will appreciate it!

Hotels, nightclubs and licensed karaoke venues in Sydney's CBD, extending across the city and into parts of Surry Hills and Kings Cross, are subject to lockout laws, which means you can't get into the venue after 1.30am and last drinks are served at 3am. Small bars don't fall under these laws.

WI-FI

Your best chance at finding free Wi-Fi in Sydney is at hotels, cafes and public libraries. Make sure your hotel has free Wi-Fi before you book! You can also get free Wi-Fi on Sydney Ferries.

The formerly industrial suburbs of Alexandria and Rosebery, in Sydney's inner south, are positively brimming with cool. It's during the day that these suburbs come alive, as the precinct houses some of the top homewares stores and cafes in the city. You'll have to hunt them down among industrial estates, factories, residential buildings and developments – but that's all part of the fun.

If you're looking to grab a coffee on the go and sit somewhere lush and lovely, take a walk to nearby Sydney Park, where you can make like a Sydneysider and soak up the sun.

SHOP
1 Koskela

EAT
2 Black Star Pastry
3 No. 12 Trading

EAT AND DRINK
4 The Grounds of Alexandria
5 Salt Meats Cheese

ALEXANDRIA AND ROSEBERY

COPELAND STREET

FOUNTAIN STREET

Erskineville Oval

DON CAMPOS

Alexandria Park

WATERLOO

ROSETTA STONE ARTISAN BAKERY

BOTANY

MCEVOY

STREET

MITCHELL

BREAD & CIRCUS WHOLEFOODS CANTEEN

MCEVOY STREET

WYNDHAM STREET

Waterloo Park

ELIZABETH STREET

ROAD

CAFE WITHOUT A NAME

STREET

N

Creek

BOURKE

EUSTON ROAD

ALEXANDRIA

ROAD

GREEN SQUARE

ZETLAND

HUNTLEY STREET

Sheas

BOURKE

ROAD

Perry Park

STREET

ROAD

JOYNTON AVENUE

THE GROUNDS OF ALEXANDRIA

ROAD

O'RIORDAN

RESERVE STREET

COCO REPUBLIC

EPSOM ROAD

Alexandra Canal

COLLINS

BEACONSFIELD

SALT MEATS CHEESE

CLICKON FURNITURE

TO NO. 12 TRADING (SEE MAP LEFT)

BOURKE

CRESSY STREET

STREET

ALEXANDRIA HOMEMAKER CENTRE

STREET

STREET

AVENUE

AVENUE

AVENUE

0   200 m

BOTANY

O'RIORDAN

DUNNING

KOSKELA

ROSEBERY

MATT BLATT

ROAD

HAYES

SOKOL

BLACK STAR PASTRY

ROSEBERY

ROTHSCHILD ROAD

HARCOURT

Turruwul Park

GARDENERS ROAD

BOTANY

GARDENERS

PARADE

ROAD

1.

KOSKELA
1/85 Dunning Ave, Rosebery
9200 0999
koskela.com.au
Open Mon–Fri 9am–5pm,
Sat 9am–4pm, Sun 10am–4pm

Set in a mammoth warehouse space flooded with natural light, furniture-and-decor store Koskela is more than a showroom – it's a revelation! The focus is on furniture that's ethically produced and designed to last. You won't find pieces like this elsewhere; take the stunning PAMPA rugs, for example, or the Polska stools made from recyclable polyethylene. Koskela has been going strong for 16 years and runs regular workshops on topics like ceramics, origami, carving and fabric dyeing. There's also an on-site cafe, which is a great spot for a pre-shopping breakfast.

2.

BLACK STAR PASTRY

C1, 85–113 Dunning Ave,
Rosebery
9700 8585
blackstarpastry.com.au
Open Mon–Fri 8am–3pm,
Sat–Sun 8am–4pm

Queues at Black Star's
Newtown venue go out the
door and up the street some
days, so it made perfect sense
when the bakery opened up
a Rosebery branch in 2014
to spread its magic beyond
the flagship store. Strawberry
watermelon cake with
rose-scented cream, amedei
chocolate and hazelnut
torte … The stand-out treats
at this industrial little bakery-
cum-cafe will inspire awe
(and gluttony!) Pop in for a
cino and a cheeky treat or stay
for a full meal. The lamb shank
pie is highly recommended.

NO 12. TRADING
12 Lenthall St, Kensington
9662 2989
no12trading.com.au
Open Mon–Fri 7am–4pm,
Sat 8am–4pm, Sun 9am–3pm

Nestled just outside of Rosebery in the bordering suburb of Kensington, No.12 Trading serves both nosh and nostalgia. Grab a coffee, a sweet or savoury treat, and mosey the antiques and repurposed relics of this cafe-cum-vintage emporium. If you'd prefer a sit-down snack, don't forget to scope the table – it's for sale too! It doesn't get any quainter.

HOT TIP
You simply must take a whiff of No. 12's unique candle range, which is absolute nirvana for the nostrils!

4.

THE GROUNDS OF ALEXANDRIA

Building 7A, 2 Huntley St,
Alexandria
9699 2225
thegrounds.com.au
Open Mon–Fri 7am–4pm,
Sat–Sun 7.30am–4pm

With stellar coffee, delicious healthy fare, a vegetable garden and resident farmyard animals, it's easy to see why this heritage-listed cafe is often busier than a Boxing Day sale. The Grounds pairs unbeatable brews – refined in the on-site coffee research facility – with hearty and wholesome daytime bites (organic, free-range, gluten-free). Heirloom tomatoes – picked fresh from the garden – play with poached eggs, double-smoked ham, fetta and pesto at breakfast, while lunch might deliver a ground beef brisket burger or crab bruschetta. Sitting down is completely optional; The Grounds is at its best in summer when you can wander the food and flower markets, sip fresh lemonade, marvel at the communal atmosphere and say hi to the chickens and local celeb pig, Kevin Bacon.

HOT TIP

Looking to try something interactive and fun? Salt Meats Cheese run regular classes in mozzarella making, pizza and pasta prep and lots more.

SALT MEATS CHEESE
41 Bourke Road, Alexandria
9319 2974
saltmeatscheese.com.au
Open Mon–Sun 9am–6pm

Salt Meats Cheese is an Italian providore warehouse filled with imported foods that you can dine in or out on. The front bench is packed with giant cheese wheels and cured porks, and you can sit on a stool and enjoy some of the gourmet selection. Head further into the warehouse and you'll hit the salt counter, where you can sample and buy every type of salt imaginable – with shakers on-hand for taste testing. This mecca also sells stuffed peppers, olives, dips and just about every other antipasti plate inclusion you could dream up. It's the place to go for an indulgent food fill.

Jessi Deakin has worked in the fashion industry in Alexandria for years. She's also the talented creative behind Sydney brand Dreamcatcher Designs, which produces macramé home decor, and is a qualified interior stylist and self-confessed cake aficionado.

Where does a local get good coffee?

I don't know anyone in the office who would pass up a cup from Campos Coffee in Alexandria. It's part of a trendy little food hub on Fountain Street and is neighbours with Bread & Circus Wholefoods Canteen and Rosetta Stone Artisan Bakery. It's the perfect one-stop shop for quality coffee and a bite to eat.

Where's the best place to grab lunch?

There is an adorable little cafe in McCauley Street, Alexandria called Cafe Without a Name. Each week it has a new and exciting 'jaffle of the week'. As the space is shared with a hardware store, the interior is quite literally industrial – and you can sit outside and enjoy your lunch on a table built from pallets.

What are the best stores to spend some money in?

Alexandria and Rosebery are amazing for homewares and furniture shopping. Clickon Furniture, Matt Blatt, Coco Republic, Sokol and other design meccas are all within a few minutes of each other. And there's also the Alexandria Homemaker Centre nearby.

Where do you go to relax outside Sydney?

Anywhere on the New South Wales south coast for me; Milton, Berry, Huskisson. These places are all so beautiful, peaceful and quaint and have the most adorable independent shops and restaurants owned by the locals. I love the friendly coastal community vibe.

BALMAIN AND ROZELLE

These two historically working class but now very-much yuppie suburbs in Sydney's Inner West sit on their own little peninsula crammed with terraced houses and old docks. Locals have largely moved on from blue collars to yoga pants, but the precinct hasn't lost its strong sense of past and identity. With history and harbour views around every corner (plus a bustling foodie scene), you'll never want to leave.

The two suburbs form a large enclave, but you can still explore them both in a day. Stick to the main strip – Darling Street – and you won't go wrong. Start in Rozelle near the Essential Ingredient and work your way down towards Balmain.

24   JUN 8876

SHOP
1 HOME INDUSTRY
2 PENNY FARTHING DESIGN HOUSE
3 THE ESSENTIAL INGREDIENT

17

EAT
4 BELLE FLEUR
EAT AND DRINK
5 THE COTTAGE
6 WILHELMINA'S
DRINK
7 THE LODGE

COCKATOO
ISLAND

River

Robinsons
Point

Yurulbin
Point

Yurulbin
Park

Parramatta

Birchgrove
Park

Snails
Bay

BIRCHGROVE

Ballast
Point

STREET

Ballast
Point Park

ROWNTREE

Mort Bay
Park

Mort
Bay

Simmons
Point

THE
LODGE

DARLING

STREET

THE
COTTAGE
WILHELMINA'S

THE
HUNTER
WORKS

⊕ STEM

KAFEINE ⊕ DARLING

PENNY
FARTHING
DESIGN
HOUSE

BALMAIN
EAST

HOME
INDUSTRY

BEATTIE

STREET

STREET

STREET

BALMAIN

STREET

ADOLPHUS STREET

Camarons
Cove

⊕
EUFORIA

HYAM STREET

DONNELLY

STREET

STREET

Johnsons
Bay

MULLENS

Pirrama
Park

STREET

White
Bay

GLEBE
ISLAND

ROBERT

ROZELLE

TO
THE ESSENTIAL
INGREDIENT
(SEE MAP LEFT)

WESTERN

JOHN STREET
SQUARE

STAR
CITY

DISTRIBUTOR

Anzac Bridge

PYRMONT

0   200 m

N

1.

HOME INDUSTRY

62 Darling St, Balmain East
0818 4524
homeindustry.com.au
Open Tues–Fri 10am–5pm,
Sat 9am–2pm

- -

Run by a mum and two-daughter team, Home Industry is located in a charming heritage building that was once a bakery. It still houses the original bakery rooms, so expect to see a few rustic ovens if you look into their workshop space (where they also host upholstery classes). This charming store specialises in furniture restoration, reupholstering and vintage homewares. It has gorgeous cloth fabric you can purchase by the metre and an interior design service from local decorator, Kate Connor. Just be warned: once you step into this fabric wonderland, it's mighty hard to pull yourself back out.

2.

PENNY FARTHING DESIGN HOUSE

51 Darling St, Balmain East
8068 6321
pennyfarthingdh.com.au
Open Mon, Tues, Thurs & Fri
10am–2pm, Sat 10am– 4pm

- -

There's no better place in Sydney to find art than the Penny Farthing Design House. This place is all about showcasing the work of local artists and allowing you to put said art in your pad at a reasonable price. There are no local artists that the lady behind the biz, Sarah Neilsen, isn't aware of. It's that sort of finger-on-the-pulse approach that makes this house so special. The showroom itself is an interior design delight filled with original art, prints, maps and photographs.

HOT TIP
Self catering? Check out
the Essential Ingredient's
gourmet grocery area

THE ESSENTIAL INGREDIENT
731–735 Darling St, Rozelle
9555 8300
sydneyessential.com.au
Open Mon–Wed & Fri
9.30am–5.30pm, Thurs
9.30am–7pm, Sat 9am–5pm,
Sun 10am–4pm

A mecca for food lovers from
all walks of life, The Essential
Ingredient is a Rozelle triple
treat. It comprises a store jam-
packed with everything you
need in the kitchen, a cafe
serving up a selection of tasty
treats and a cooking school
where you can learn to make
anything and everything from
Thai and Mexican dishes to
pasta or paella. The staff have
an obvious passion for food
that's rubbed off on the locals.
It's always busy and there's
always something on, so if
you're dying to know how to
make duck in three different
ways, there's a class that has
you covered!

4.

BELLE FLEUR
658 Darling Street, Rozelle
9810 2690
bellefleur.com.au
Open Mon–Fri 9am–6pm,
Sat 9am–5pm, Sun 10am–4pm

As soon as you open the
glass doors to Belle Fleur, the
waft of Belgian chocolate
hits your nostrils. No, this
isn't heaven – just the skill of
four generations of chocolate
makers at work. And the
fun doesn't stop at one bite;
sink your teeth into one of
Belle Fleur's fine chocolate
gift boxes, which start at
11 pieces and go up to 64 (just
get the 64-piece box and call
it a day!). You get to choose
the make-up of your gift box,
too. It's pretty hard to say
no to a handmade chocolate
store as good as this one.

HOT TIP
Get some drinking
chocolate, too. The bags
are super affordable and
taste truly amazing.

THE COTTAGE
342 Darling St, Balmain
8084 8185
thecottagebalmain.com.au
Open Mon–Wed 5pm–late,
Thurs–Sat 12pm–12am,
Sun 12pm–10pm

Most bars house their garden areas at the back of the venue, but The Cottage shows you its hand the moment you pull up outside. With a leafy drinking spot out front of the historical sandstone building, you'll definitely be able to see yourself enjoying a drink or two under the fairy lights. Inside, the feeling is vintage farmhouse and the menu features share plates like prawn cakes or a charcuterie board, as well as an entire oven-fired pizza menu, ideal for groups. This is the perfect spot to sit back with a drink and survey the day's purchases.

6.

WILHELMINA'S

332 Darling St, Balmain
8068 8762
wilhelminas.com.au
Open Tues–Fri 5pm–late,
Sat–Sun 8am–late

Wilhelmina's is an all-day venue that does day into night right – put it down to their seasonal menu, the local booze and fit-out. The menu is ever-changing but the ethos is always about keeping it fresh and using produce from small-hold farmers. Add to that the range of local craft beer and organic boutique wine and you have an around-the-clock culinary winner. When it comes to the decor, that too gets the thumbs-up. Look out for the stunning Anya Brock mural that dominates one of the walls – it's truly something.

7.

THE LODGE

3/415 Darling St, Balmain
0004 2502
thelodgebar.com.au
Open Tues–Wed 4–10pm,
Thurs–Sat 4–11pm,
Sun 12–5pm

The Lodge is an intimate little bar, all calm and charm, with candles flickering of an evening and jazz and blues music wafting through the air (no need to yell at your companions to have a conversation here). Its old rococo chairs, studded-leather seating and dapper atmosphere can make a guy feel a little James Bond–ish. Don't be surprised if you get the urge to order a scotch on the rocks, but then you'd be passing up the extensive wine list (which goes beautifully with the bar's dreamy cheese board). There's nothing else like this in Balmain.

Lucy Sutherland is exposed to creativity around the clock. Not only is she the general manager of the International School of Colour & Design, she's also a managing consultant for trend forecasting giant, Colourways. She's lived in Balmain for years, so was the perfect person to ask about the best places to seek out in the area.

Where will we find you having breakfast?

We are so spoilt for choice in this area. One of my favourites would be Kafeine in Balmain: great coffee, great space, amazing vibe and, of course, really good food. I also love the Hunter Works, an undercover courtyard cafe down an alleyway just off Balmain's Darling Street.

What are your favourite places to shop?

Stem, right in the hub of Balmain, is a great place for last-minute gifts, gorgeous Scandinavian-inspired homewares and stunning jewellery. Penny Farthing Design House in Balmain East (*see* page 014) is an essential go-to destination for art. I walk my dogs past its window most mornings and am always obsessing over at least one of its pieces!

Can you recommend some amazing dinner spots in the area?

Wilhelmina's (*see* page 018) is a welcome addition to the Balmain dining scene. The Lodge (*see* page 018) is another hidden gem on Darling Street. It is a perfect winter venue with deep leather lounges, low lighting and dark timber panelling.

What do you do on a day out in the area?

There are so many gorgeous parks and little enclaves that allow you to forget that you're in the middle of the city. I love to walk to Illoura Reserve at the end of Darling Street, grab a coffee from Euforia, and then wander down to the harbourside park. I enjoy people-watching, from the group of ladies doing yoga every Saturday with their golden retrievers looking on, to the constant run of ferries and kayaks meandering past.

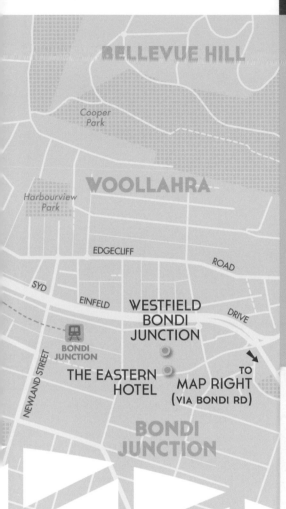

Bondi is the most iconic suburb in Sydney, and the beach has everything to do with it. The locals here are so fit and healthy – it's hard not to get swept up in their zest for life. Take a deep breath of sea air and throw yourself into the action.

It's jam-packed of a weekend with a mix of tourists and locals enjoying a swim or a surf. If you need a break from the crowds, there are lots of stores and eateries to explore away from the beach, but be prepared for a few uphill climbs. The views from the cliff-tops are world famous, so get ready to lose your breath in more ways than one. Try the Bondi to Bronte coastal walk, a fabulous 6 kilometre stroll which starts next to the Bondi Icebergs Club (*see* page 030).

24   JUN 8016

ʃHOP
1 BONDI MARKETS
2 BONDI ʃHOPPING

17

EAT
3 DA ORAZIO PIZZA &
    PORCHETTA
4 ʃHUK
5 NORTH BONDI FISH
EAT AND DRINK
6 BONDI ICEBERGS CLUB
7 THE EASTERN HOTEL

BELLEVUE HILL

Cooper Park

WOOLLAHRA

Harbourview Park

EDGECLIFF

ROAD

SYD

EINFELD

DRIVE

WESTFIELD
BONDI
JUNCTION

BONDI
JUNCTION

NEWLAND STREET

THE EASTERN
HOTEL

TO
MAP RIGHT
(VIA BONDI RD)

BONDI
JUNCTION

BONDI

QUEENS PARK ROAD

VICTORIA STREET

BRONTE ROAD

CARRINGTON ROAD

Queens Park

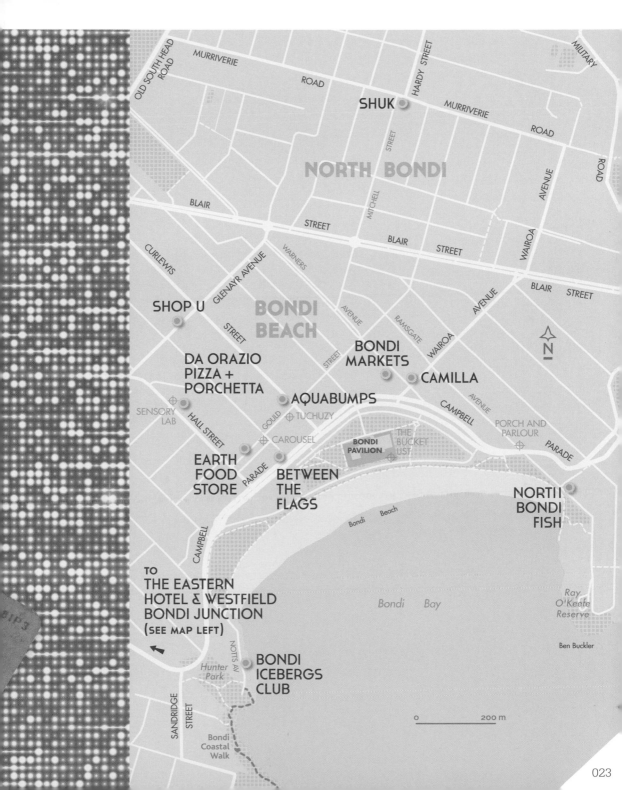

SHUK

NORTH BONDI

MURRIVERIE ROAD
OLD SOUTH HEAD ROAD
HARDY STREET
MURRIVERIE ROAD
MILITARY ROAD
STREET
MITCHELL STREET
AVENUE
WAIROA ROAD

BLAIR STREET
BLAIR STREET
BLAIR STREET
WARNERS AVENUE

CURLEWIS
GLENAYR AVENUE
RAMSGATE AVENUE
WAIROA AVENUE

BONDI BEACH

SHOP U

DA ORAZIO PIZZA + PORCHETTA

BONDI MARKETS

CAMILLA

AQUABUMPS

CAMPBELL AVENUE

PORCH AND PARLOUR

SENSORY LAB

HALL STREET

GOULD STREET
TUCHUZY
CAROUSEL

CAMPBELL PARADE

BONDI PAVILION

THE BUCKET LIST

PARADE

EARTH FOOD STORE

BETWEEN THE FLAGS

NORTH BONDI FISH

Bondi Beach

CAMPBELL PARADE

Ray O'Keefe Reserve

TO THE EASTERN HOTEL & WESTFIELD BONDI JUNCTION (SEE MAP LEFT)

Bondi Bay

Ben Buckler

NOTTS AV

Hunter Park

BONDI ICEBERGS CLUB

SANDRIDGE STREET

Bondi Coastal Walk

0   200 m

023

1.

BONDI MARKETS

Bondi Beach Public School,
Campbell Pde, Bondi Beach
9315 7011
bondimarkets.com.au
Open Sat 9am–1pm,
Sun 10am–4pm

The Bondi Markets have been going strong since 1993, so they've well and truly become part of the local routine. A wander through is a great way to get a taste of these lucky locals' seaside lifestyle. Come on Saturday for the farmers' market with its abundance of fruit and veg, dairy produce, essential oils, green products and more – all of which just might explain why the locals shopping alongside you look so healthy. Of a Sunday, things are less food-focused, with artisans showcasing the best in local clothing, jewellery, art, decor and crafts. You can meet the local designers who make the products, and get a friend or family member a gift you can't find anywhere else!

2.

BONDI SHOPPING
See map

Bondi is an undeniable sun and surf mecca but there are also some amazing boutique shops to explore along the beach. Homewares lovers should make a beeline for **Shop U** (Glenayr Avenue), which is filled with designer lighting, wallpaper, cushions and more. If art is your thing, **Aquabumps** (Curlewis Street) sells photographs of the beach. Join the seaside glam set with a floaty designer kaftan from **Camilla** (Warners Avenue), or grab some iconic Bondi-branded apparel at **Between the Flags** (Campbell Parade). For a healthy snack to keep you fuelled while foraging, **Earth Food Store** (pictured, Gould Street), has your organic, gluten-free and everything-else-free needs covered.

If you want more shops, take a bus or drive to nearby Westfield Bondi Junction – it's one of the best upmarket shopping centres in Sydney.

1.

2.

HOT TIP
After a cosy post-market coffee? Try Gertrude & Alice, a charming cafe-cum-bookstore on Hall Street.

3.

DA ORAZIO PIZZA & PORCHETTA

Shop 16/19 The Hub
75–79 Hall Street, Bondi
8090 6969
daorazio.com
Open Mon–Fri 5pm–late,
Sat–Sun 12pm–late

Everything at Da Orazio screams style, from the professionally uniformed staff to the minimalist interior (all stark white, wood and rendered concrete) and carefully curated music. But there's also substance behind all that attention to aesthetics, and the food is definitely the star of the show. As its name suggests, pizza – naturally risen for 48 hours and cooked in a wood-fired oven – is one of the leading ladies. The other scene-stealer is pork, either done on the rotisserie or slow roasted. It's only available until sold out though, so get in before the show's over.

SHUK
2 Mitchell St, North Bondi
0423 199 859
shukbondi.com
Open Mon–Thurs 6am–5pm,
Fri–Sat 6am–10pm,
Sun 7am–5pm

SHUK got a fair bit of attention in 2015 when Jamie Oliver stopped by, but the locals knew how phenomenal it was years before that. SHUK is a cafe, bakery and deli; its own little marketplace situated in what was an old milk bar. It's bustling around the clock, but if you only have time for one visit, drop in of a morning when the cafe is at its best. It's drenched in sunlight during the day and the glossy white walls and timber tables are clean and bright. SHUK serves breakfast until 1pm and the menu is packed with traditional eats with an Israeli twist. Try the Beghrir pancakes or the spicy slow-cooked beans; both are sublime. Dinner of a Friday or Saturday night is also recommended – you can't go past the braised lamb shoulder.

5.

NORTH BONDI FISH
120 Ramsgate Ave,
North Bondi
9130 2155
northbondifish.com.au
Open Wed–Sun 12pm–late

There's nothing better than overlooking the beach while you dine. You can expect to get that and more when you visit North Bondi Fish. Request a spot outside if there's one available – you can literally jump off the deck and hit the sand. The decor is inspired by the beach surrounds but doesn't go too literal, instead using texture to make the space feel inviting (polished concrete floors topped with eclectic floor rugs make for a lovely design moment). The menu is completely seafood focused; share the roast cod curry – it's fiery and fragrant! Embrace everything this stunning venue has to offer.

6.

BONDI ICEBERGS CLUB
1 Notts Ave, Bondi Beach
9130 3120
icebergs.com.au
Open Mon–Fri 11am–late,
Sat–Sun 9am–late

It would be practically criminal to come to Sydney and not experience Bondi Icebergs Club, a winter swimming club whose clubhouse overlooks ocean pools and the beach beyond. This place draws people in droves – both locals and tourists – to dine, drink and take in the postcard-perfect views (don't forget your camera). Best of all, the clubhouse bistro prices are pretty reasonable, which is surprising given the location. Tuck into a pot of black mussels, cooked in tomato, garlic, chilli and white wine. Or go for something classic like beer-battered flathead with salad and fries. There's a kids' menu, too, so this place is great for all the family.

HOT TIP
Bring your swimmers. A dip in the ocean pool is an iconic Sydney experience.

7.

THE EASTERN HOTEL
500 Oxford St, Bondi Junction
9387 7828
theeastern.com.au
Opening hours vary by venue;
see website for details

Epic is the only way to
describe this multi-level
building, which houses
four different venues for
four different experiences.
GoodTime Burgers is on
the ground floor and is the
place for classic pub grub
with a side of sports. On
level one you'll find **Bondi
Harvest**, which focuses on
healthy dining using local
produce. **El Topo Basement**
is, confusingly, on the third
level; this nightclub isn't
for the faint-hearted. At the
top of the tower, **El Topo
Mexican** is hands-down the
best of the lot, with food and
a lively rooftop atmosphere
to rival the real deal in
Central America.

HOT TIP
This hotel is attached to Bondi Junction Westfield, so it's a great spot for a post-shopping drink.

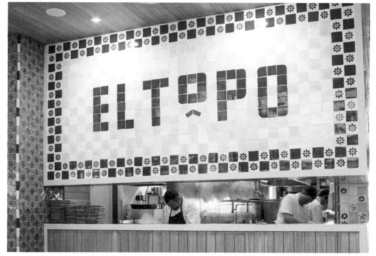

033

Jess Robinson is a Bondi girl through and through. As the personal trainer behind popular blog Lazy Girl Fitness, she divides her time between sweating it out by the beach and eating out around it. A writer by trade, Jess is a dog lover who knows a good venue when she sees it.

What are the best places for a drink around Bondi?

If you're after an elegant evening, sipping perfectly mixed cocktails while surrounded by beautiful people, it's hard to go past Icebergs Dining Room & Bar (*see* page 030). If you're looking for something a little more laid-back, and where your drinking buddy can be your dog, then the Bucket List at the Bondi Pavilion (Queen Elizabeth Drive) is the way to go.

Can you recommend any foolproof breakfast destinations?

Aaaah, there are so many! I'm a massive fan of Porch & Parlour in North Bondi – it has amazing breakfast bowls, Will & Co coffee and a super-chilled vibe. Ruby's Diner up on Bronte Road is awesome too – its breakfast menu is seriously good. And if it's just coffee you're after, you can't go past Sensory Lab on Hall Street.

Where does a local go clothes shopping?

I get around in my gym gear most of the time, but when I do decide it's time to dress like a lady, Carousel or Tuchuzy have my vote.

Where do you go to get away from it all?

I'm a country girl at heart, so I head up to Grafton on the north coast to visit my family whenever possible. It used to be that you had to be in a big city to access awesome, healthy cafes, but I love that there are more and more popping up all over the place now. When I'm in Grafton, I head to Heart & Soul Wholefood Cafe for a coffee, lunch or raw treat.

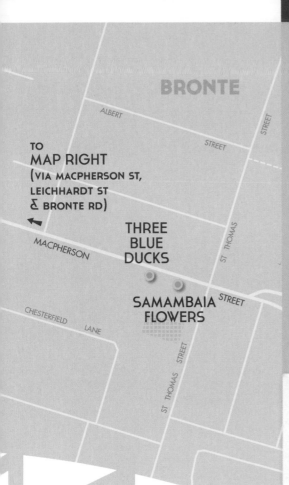

BRONTE

ALBERT STREET

STREET

TO
MAP RIGHT
(VIA MACPHERSON ST,
LEICHHARDT ST
& BRONTE RD)

MACPHERSON

THREE
BLUE
DUCKS

ST THOMAS

CHESTERFIELD LANE

SAMAMBAIA
FLOWERS

STREET

ST THOMAS STREET

ST THOMAS STREET

You'll be charmed by the neighbouring eastern suburbs of Bronte and Waverley. These suburbs are possibly the friendliest precincts in Sydney and all the locals seem to be high on life – perhaps because of their close proximity to the ocean, or maybe because their quaint homes are nestled on such beautiful, tree-lined streets.

The shops and eating venues are in pockets, so a car or bus is your friend – unless you're feeling particularly sporty. And be prepared for a few hill climbs. The obvious attraction is Bronte Beach. It's smaller and quieter than Bondi or Coogee's beaches, but just as picturesque. The ocean pool is a great spot for swimming and a nice escape from pretty rough surf.

24   JUN 6076

SHOP
1 The Bronte Tram
2 The Design Hunter
3 Samambaia

17

EAT
4 Bronte Road Bistro
5 Three Blue Ducks
EAT AND DRINK
6 Charing Cross Hotel

BRONTE
AND WAVERLEY

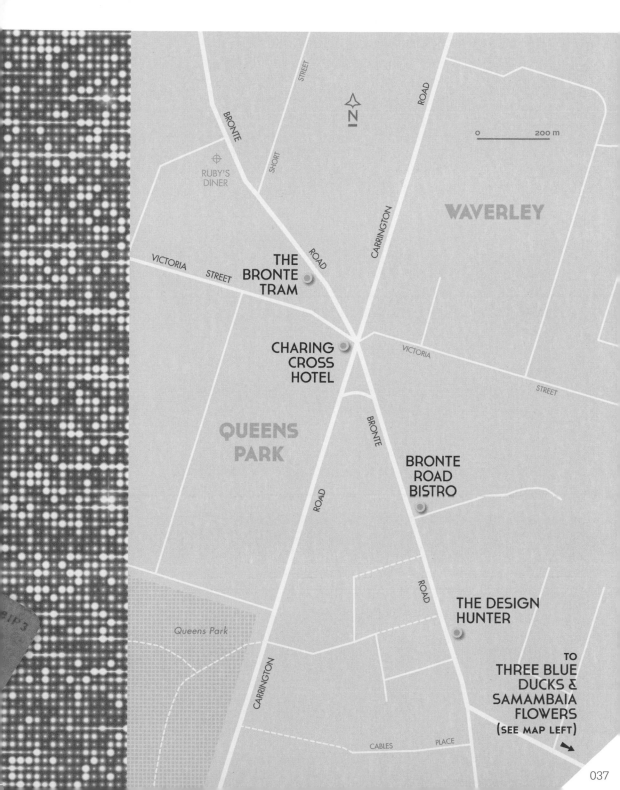

STREET

BRONTE

SHORT

ROAD

RUBY'S DINER

N

CARRINGTON

ROAD

WAVERLEY

0   200 m

VICTORIA   STREET

THE BRONTE TRAM

CHARING CROSS HOTEL

VICTORIA

STREET

BRONTE

QUEENS PARK

BRONTE ROAD BISTRO

ROAD

ROAD

THE DESIGN HUNTER

CARRINGTON

Queens Park

TO
THREE BLUE DUCKS &
SAMAMBAIA
FLOWERS
(SEE MAP LEFT)

CABLES   PLACE

1.

THE BRONTE TRAM

195 Bronte Rd, Waverley
9389 1337
facebook.com/
thebrontetramsydney
Open Mon–Sat 10am–5pm,
Sun 11am–4pm

This destination for all things antique was named after an old tram that used to cut through Bronte on its way to Bondi. The tram has long since stopped operating, but other reminders of yesteryear are very much in the here and now at this fascinating shop (original Indian wedding chest, anyone?). After an hour in the jam-packed store, you might have picked up apothecary bottles, aged mirrors, character-laden leather suitcases, vintage jelly and chocolate moulds, copper pots, typewriters, old clocks, chandeliers, globes, you name it. Original antique furniture, including gorgeous French and Japanese pieces, also make an appearance, and there are usually a few rocking horses and old teddy bears for sale that walk a fine line between stunning and spooky.

2.

THE DESIGN HUNTER

316 Bronte Rd, Waverley
9369 3322
thedesignhunter.com.au
Open Mon–Sun 10am–5pm

With a retail shop, design service and online store, it's safe to say that the Design Hunter is the go-to style destination in this area. Its sun-filled bricks-and-mortar store feels distinctly global, with all the latest interior trends showcased inside. The style of the products would be best described as coastal with a generous nod to a rustic, tribal aesthetic, with every corner of the store carefully curated by its talented showroom consultants. Find Armadillo & Co rugs mixed in with travel candles, ceramic jugs, leather journals and Icelandic sheepskin throws. It's a hard store to pigeon-hole, which is probably why it's so popular with locals.

1.

2.

2.

1.

1.

THE
BRONTE TRAM

SPEECH PATHOLOGY &
OCCUPATIONAL THERAPY
PH 9389 3322

2.

3.

SAMAMBAIA
145B Macpherson St, Bronte
9389 9125
samambaiaflowers.com
Open Mon–Fri 9am–5pm,
Sat 9am–2pm

This is no run-of-the-mill florist. Recycled fence palings line the walls, and they are only the beginning of the visual treats. Owner Maria Claudia has filled her shop with the most incredible flower arrangements and other more suitcase-friendly gems, like small candles, bowls, macramé plant holders, books and glassware. The business started in Maria's old garage, but word of mouth soon allowed her to move into these premises, where she has created a Zen-like wonderland that provides an escape from the hectic foot traffic outside and a rare treat for your senses.

BRONTE ROAD BISTRO
282 Bronte Rd, Waverley
9389 3028
bronteroadbistro.com
Open Tues–Thurs
5.30–9.30pm, Fri–Sat
12–2.30pm & 5.30–9.30pm

Bronte Road Bistro was a welcome Waverley addition when it landed in 2008 and is still drawing crowds today, especially for its divine dinner service. The menu is influenced by the Mediterranean – think baked eggplant, confit duck leg and pan-fried spatchcock – and the carefully curated wine list isn't half bad, either. The staff are all pros in wine-pairing, so be sure to seek their advice when ordering. Find a seat in the courtyard as the lights dim; dining alfresco is what the locals do!

5.

THREE BLUE DUCKS
141–143 Macpherson St, Bronte
9389 0010
threeblueducks.com
Open Mon–Tues 7am–3.30pm,
Wed–Sat 7am–3pm & 6–11pm,
Sun 7am–3pm

- -

Three Blue Ducks showcases
everything that's good
about Bronte – friendliness,
community and the good life.
Started by three surfer-dude
mates, it effortlessly combines
a super-chilled atmosphere
(hello graffiti!) with knockout,
sophisticated food. The
menu might include smoked
salmon, dukkah, poached
eggs, labneh chilli and kale
for breakfast; pork belly,
kimchi, pickled cucumber,
sesame and coriander for
lunch; or barbecue-smoked
beef brisket, charred corn and
pickles for dinner. Much of
what you see on your plate
will be organic and locally
sourced (very local in some
cases – straight from the
restaurant's chemical-free
kitchen garden). What's more,
these guys are much-loved
in the community, setting
up kerbside herb gardens
that anyone can access, and
working with the locals to
compost all of the restaurant's
organic waste. So much
to love!

CHARING CROSS HOTEL
81 Carrington Rd, Waverley
9389 3093
charingcrosshotel.com.au
Open Mon–Thurs 10am–12am,
Fri–Sat 10am–2am,
Sun 10am–10pm

All praise the decor gods behind Charing Cross Hotel's refurbishment, which took place a few years back and gave it a modern Miami vibe (with a taxidermy peacock thrown in for good measure). Its new lease on life has been a hit with patrons, who flock to it for both a drink and a meal. The bold wallpaper that spans the length of the dining room takes your eye on a journey to the beer garden, which is the place to be on a sunny afternoon. While its fit-out might be fresh, the friendly vibe that's been here for years still remains. The layout is all open, with no real breaks between the bar and the dining area, so everyone gets to enjoy the atmosphere together.

Melissa Bonney knows good decor. She's the talented director behind the Design Hunter (*see page 038*), a highly regarded interior design store in Waverley that delivers more than meets the eye. Not only does she operate the interior design side of the business, she lives just down the road from the store – a true local.

What's the vibe like here?

It's a really casual, beachside community that's generally very relaxed and with an interesting mix of young and old. Many of its residents have been locals for 20 to 30 years! There's definitely a 'shop local' vibe here too.

Where do you start your morning?

We're a bit spoilt for choice these days, with so many new local places popping up. But Ruby's Diner in Waverley is definitely my go-to spot for great coffee, loose-leaf chai or kombucha tea on tap.

What's the best place for a dinner date?

You definitely can't go past Three Blue Ducks in Bronte (*see* page 042) for dinner with that someone special. It has a casual atmosphere but the most sophisticated menu that rivals all of its contemporaries.

Where do you go to get away from it all?

Noosa in Queensland is definitely top of my list. It ticks all of my boxes at the moment – warm weather, stunning beaches, great food and loads of activities for the family.

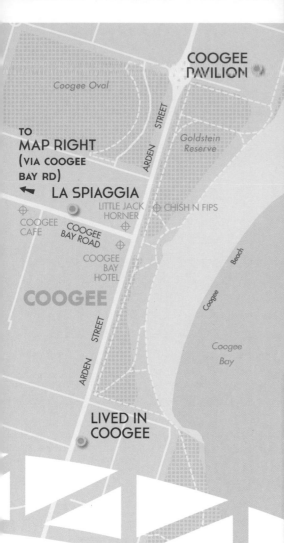

COOGEE PAVILION

Coogee Oval

ARDEN STREET

Goldstein
Reserve

TO
MAP RIGHT
(VIA COOGEE
BAY RD)
← LA SPIAGGIA

LITTLE JACK
HORNER   ⊕ CHISH N FIPS

COOGEE   COOGEE
CAFE   BAY ROAD

COOGEE
BAY
HOTEL

Coogee Beach

COOGEE

ARDEN STREET

Coogee
Bay

LIVED IN
COOGEE

COOGEE
AND RANDWICK

Neptune
Park

Blenheim
Park

Coogee and Randwick are family oriented suburbs in Sydney's east with an easy, breezy feel; dining out is anything but stuffy and the stores are filled with subdued but divine decor gems.

Exploring Coogee is easy; walk along the beach on Arden Street for some picturesque views and enjoy take-away fish and chips. Along the water it's relatively flat, but as you head up Coogee Bay Road, which is loaded with eateries, the incline up the hill towards Randwick begins. The Spot – a cluster of eateries and stores on Perouse Road – is a bustling hub of activity. It's a heritage conservation area and is home to the iconic Ritz Cinema; built in 1937 and still as remarkable today as it was back then.

24   JUN 8066

SHOP
1 HUMBLE BEGINNINGS
2 LIVE THIS
3 LIVED IN COOGEE

17

EAT AND DRINK
4 COOGEE PAVILION
5 LA SPIAGGIA
6 RANDWICK RITZ CINEMA
DRINK
7 BAT COUNTRY

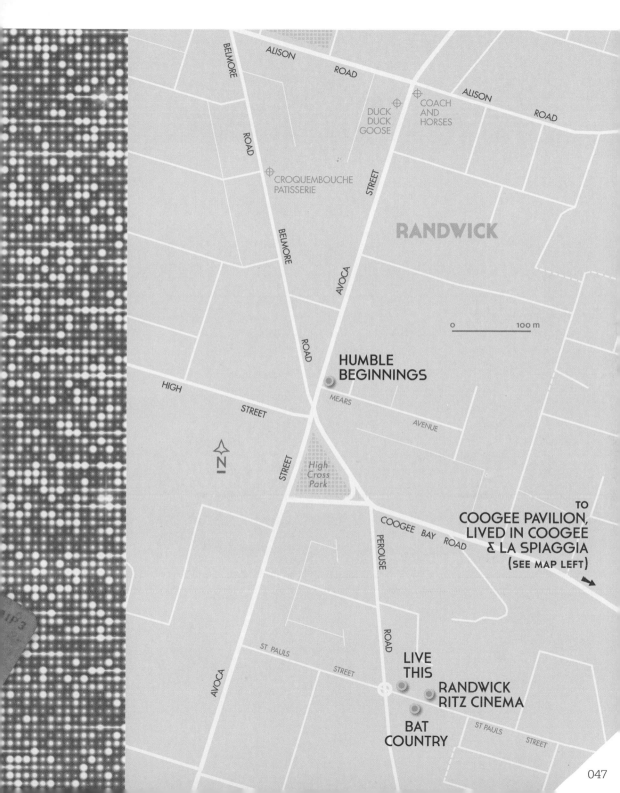

BELMORE
ALISON ROAD
ROAD
ALISON ROAD

DUCK DUCK GOOSE
COACH AND HORSES

CROQUEMBOUCHE PATISSERIE

RANDWICK

STREET

AVOCA

0   100 m

ROAD

HUMBLE BEGINNINGS

HIGH
STREET
MEARS
AVENUE

STREET

BELMORE

N

High Cross Park

COOGEE BAY ROAD

TO
COOGEE PAVILION,
LIVED IN COOGEE
& LA SPIAGGIA
(SEE MAP LEFT)

PEROUSE

ROAD

ST PAULS
STREET

AVOCA

LIVE THIS

RANDWICK RITZ CINEMA

BAT COUNTRY

ST PAULS STREET

1.

HUMBLE BEGINNINGS
209 Avoca St, Randwick
9326 4383
Open Mon–Sat 9.30am–6pm,
Sun 9.30am–5.30pm

- -

How does a shop survive these days without a website or Facebook page? Spend some time in Humble Beginnings and you'll find out. This homewares and gift haven has been a part of the community for over 20 years and its regulars have been devotees from the start. The owners have witnessed kids become adult customers and produce offspring of their own, coming back time and again for things like soaps, dinnerware, books, framed prints and ornaments. It goes to show that when a store operates with heart and history (and a touch of humility), its customers get hooked for life.

2.

LIVE THIS
33 St Pauls St, Randwick
9398 8664
livethis.bigcartel.com
Open Mon–Thurs & Sun
11am–7pm, Fri–Sat 11am–10pm

- -

Over the years, many businesses have come and gone from the Spot, a heritage conservation area in Randwick, but Live This has been there for over a decade now, with no signs of moving on. This eclectic store offers a bit of everything – homewares, gifts, jewellery, body products, women's clothing, handbags and accessories – but it's all done with absolute class. Gals go gaga over the long jewellery cabinet that runs the length of the store, and regulars return again and again for much-loved clothing brands. Most of the wares are colour-coded so you can gravitate towards your favourite hue. It's really very easy to see what makes this place a stayer.

FRESH FLOWERS AVAILABLE

Got kids or friends with kids? Humble Beginnings have a cute baby clothing and decor area you'll adore!

3.

LIVED IN COOGEE
263 Arden St, Coogee
9665 5330
livedincoogee.com.au
Open Tues–Fri 9.30am–5pm,
Sat 10am–5pm, Sun 11am–4pm

If you've never been a fan of the subdued colour palette when it comes to interiors, it will take you about four seconds in this store to become a convert. Lived in Coogee is a light-filled furniture and homewares oasis that blends coastal-, organic- and tribal-inspired pieces to perfection, things that feel global and rare. Most items are on the beige/brown/white scale and their earthiness and calming nature will have you ditching your red leather sofa in a flash. See if you can stop yourself from going home with a piece of jewellery, coasters, candles or coral. The store's tagline is 'be inspired' and you'll come away with grand visions to transform your home.

4.

COOGEE PAVILION

169 Dolphin St, Coogee
9240 3000
merivale.com.au/
coogeepavilion
Open 7.30am–late

- -

A few years ago, the Coogee Pavilion underwent cosmetic surgery and emerged from the operation as a true beachside beauty. This place is massive – like, absolutely massive – and is split over three levels. On the ground floor, the cantina-style set-up is ideal for a family feed. You can blow in from the beach – towel and all – and nosh on traditional seaside food, like freshly shucked oysters and the catch of the day. There's a huge, old-school play area out the back, with games like table tennis for kids and adults alike. The rooftop is the place to be sans young'uns. This adults-only zone comprises several bars and a wraparound balcony with killer views of the ocean (probably best to wash the sand off before heading up here).

5.

LA SPIAGGIA

248 Coogee Bay Road,
Coogee
9665 4660
laspiaggia.com.au
Open Mon–Thurs
5.30–10.30pm, Fri–Sat
5.30–11pm, 5.30–10pm

La Spiaggia is Coogee's oldest Italian restaurant and has been run by the Lombardo family for decades. The vibe is classy, yet casual, with a large dining room (excellent for group bookings). It's an authentic Italian feed where the food is the star of the show. The menu is packed full of pizza, pasta and a range of mains; standouts include the tenderised veal cutlet, free-range roasted half duck and the seafood casserole. They also have a take-away menu so you can enjoy nonna-approved meals back at your accommodation.

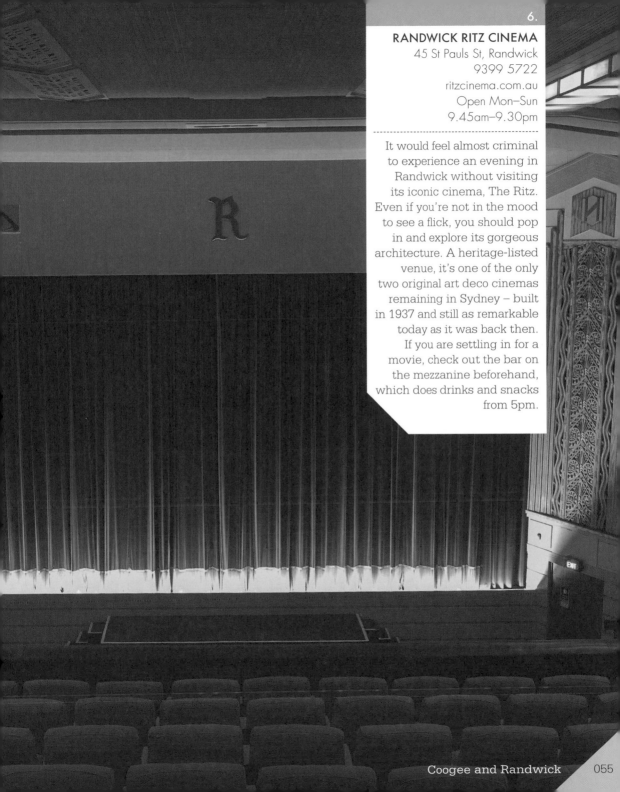

RANDWICK RITZ CINEMA
45 St Pauls St, Randwick
9399 5722
ritzcinema.com.au
Open Mon–Sun
9.45am–9.30pm

It would feel almost criminal to experience an evening in Randwick without visiting its iconic cinema, The Ritz. Even if you're not in the mood to see a flick, you should pop in and explore its gorgeous architecture. A heritage-listed venue, it's one of the only two original art deco cinemas remaining in Sydney – built in 1937 and still as remarkable today as it was back then. If you are settling in for a movie, check out the bar on the mezzanine beforehand, which does drinks and snacks from 5pm.

7.

BAT COUNTRY
32 St Pauls St, Randwick
9398 6694
batcountry.com.au
Open Mon–Sat 7am–12am,
Sun 7am–10pm

Locals must have lost their minds when Bat Country landed in Randwick a few years ago; it finally gave the suburb a hip and happening watering hole to call its own. Cafe by day and bustling bar by night, the venue is inspired by legendary author Hunter S. Thompson, with a mural of the man himself in their beer garden. The cosy, exposed-brick-wall interior gives a generous nod to vintage decor (think rattan chairs, padded leather booths and old lampshades), with mixologists on hand who'll be more than happy to recommend their fave knock-your-socks-off libation. If you're around during the day, pop in for breakfast or lunch. Their bacon and egg roll with hot sauce is sublime.

HOT TIP
You'll be busting to see the toilet walls covered from floor to ceiling in art.

Adam Murphy has been an animator for 25 years and has a CV boasting employers like Disney and Lucasfilm, to name just a couple. Who better to suggest some cool and creative venues in the area that you simply must visit?

What's the vibe like in these suburbs?

They're so close and yet so different: it's chilled and rambling down at Coogee Beach, while up the hill at Randwick things are fast and tight.

Where's the best place to grab lunch?

The Coogee Bay Hotel and Barzura, both in Coogee, have great menus and sea breezes. Or grab something from Chish N Fips, also in Coogee, and take it down to the beach – but make sure you watch out for the chip-pinching seagulls!

Where's a great spot for an evening drink?

The Coach & Horses in Randwick is a great old hotel. Or grab a drink upstairs before a movie at Randwick's Ritz Cinema (*see* page 055).

Can you suggest some must-visit cafes?

The Coogee Cafe on the main drag and Little Jack Horner down on the beach are great. In Randwick, Duck Duck Goose and Croquembouche Patisserie are cosy places for a brew.

Where do you go to escape the city?

As far south as possible! It's great to get down to the Illawarra and Southern Highlands regions. I love the escarpment, sea and villages down that way.

These suburbs, just east of the city, are fashionable sisters with different personalities. Darlinghurst is more mischievous (Darlo to the locals) and Paddington is more stylish. Both suburbs are snug, with narrow streets, old terrace houses and plenty of fashionable foot traffic, and offer so much in the way of dining, shopping and entertainment.

You can easily spend an entire day in the precinct: start on the Paddington end of Oxford Street, and shop till you drop at the many boutiques, then take a break at a cafe or gallery. For a night of fun and folly, continue on to Taylor Square. It's the epicentre of Sydney's LGBT culture and comes alive at night – and especially during Mardi Gras each March.

Map labels

- PARK STREET
- STREET
- STREET
- CROSS CITY TUNNEL
- MAP RIGHT (VIA WILLIAM ST)
- Hyde Park
- ELIZABETH
- COLLEGE
- RED LILY
- MUSEUM
- LOVE TILLY DEVINE
- LIVERPOOL STREET
- EDITION COFFEE ROASTERS
- WENTWORTH AVENUE
- OXFORD
- DISTRIBUTOR
- EASTERN
- WHEELS & DOLLBABY
- CAMPBELL
- STREET
- STREET
- SURRY HILLS
- FLINDERS STREET
- ALBION
- FOVEAUX
- STREET
- STREET

DARLINGHURST AND PADDINGTON

- REDFERN
- CLEVELAND STREET
- SOUTH DOWLING STREET
- ANZAC PARADE

24 JUN 8076

SHOP
1 Oxford Street Shopping
2 Wheels & Dollbaby
EAT
3 Buffalo Dining Club
4 Edition Coffee Roasters

17

DRINK
5 Darlo Bar
6 Darlinghurst and Paddington Nightlife
7 Print Room

TO
LOVE TILLY DEVINE,
WHEELS & DOLLBABY
& EDITION COFFEE
ROASTERS
(SEE MAP LEFT)

ELIZABETH
BAY

*Rushcutters
Bay*

KINGS
CROSS

WILLIAM STREET

GREENKNOWE AVENUE

MACLEAY STREET

WARD AVENUE

RUSHCUTTERS
BAY

BAYSWATER ROAD

NEW BEACH ROAD

NEW SOUTH HEAD ROAD

EASTERN DISTRIBUTOR

ROAD STREET

BUFFALO
DINING
CLUB

DARLO
BAR

GREEN
PARK
HOTEL

DARLINGHURST

MCLACHLAN AV

AVENUE

NEILD

DARLINGHURST

VICTORIA

STREET

BROWN STREET

ROAD

MILK
DAY SPA

GLENMORE

*Trumper
Park*

CASCADE STREET

BOUNDARY

OXFORD

GLENMORE

PRINT
ROOM

ZIMMERMAN

WILLOW
APPAREL

PADDINGTON

FOUR IN
HAND

HARGRAVE

CARL
KAPP

STREET

SCANLAN
THEODORE

SASS &
BIDE

INCU

OPUS
DESIGN
CO

THE LONDON
HOTEL

STREET

VICTORIA
BARRACKS

DINOSAUR
DESIGNS

PADDINGTON
INN

PARK

N

ANZAC

*Moore
Park*

OXFORD

*Kippax
Lake*

ROAD

ANYA
BROCK

QUEEN STREET

STREET

ALLIANZ
STADIUM

0   200 m

PARADE

*Tramway
Oval*

SYDNEY
CRICKET
GROUND

MOORE
PARK

LANG ROAD

*Centennial
Park*

THE
ENTERTAINMENT
QUARTER

1.

OXFORD STREET SHOPPING

International celebs stop to shop on Oxford Street when they visit and here's why. It's packed with phenomenal Aussie art, fashion and homewares – not to mention that so many of the stores are housed within converted terrace houses (an architectural dream for lovers of historic design).

For clothing, you can't go past boutiques like **Sass & Bide**, **Carl Kapp** or **Scanlan Theodore**. Or try **Zimmerman** and **Willow Apparel** (both on nearby Glenmore Road). **Dinosaur Designs** is a must-do (started by local ladies back in 1983), with out-of-this-world resin jewellery and a host of homewares and decorative items to boot.

Anya Brock is a very talented Perth creative and produces bright abstract art you'll want a piece of (there are smaller works here that'll fit in a suitcase). **Opus Design Co.** sells fun and cheeky homewares you can give as gifts.

If you're after a facial in Paddington, **Milk Day Spa** (Glenmore Road) is the place to get it. After a day exploring the design mecca that is Oxford Street, you might need one!

WHEELS & DOLLBABY

259 Crown Street, Darlinghurst
9301 3280
wheelsanddollbaby.com
Open Mon–Sun 9am–6pm

Everyone in Sydney knows Wheels & Dollbaby. In recent years the iconic brand has gone global, with many Hollywood starlets owning clothing from this unassuming treasure chest. When you walk inside this glam rock 'n' roll clothing store, the vibe is incredibly down to earth. Established in 1987, this boutique has a range that is predominantly female-skewed. Expect to pick up wonderfully fitted dresses, pencil and mini skirts, biker jackets, leopard print fur coats and even some racy intimates. For guys, it's limited to some tees and shirts. Though the celebs are all over this brand, it's perfect for the everyday fashionista too!

BUFFALO DINING CLUB
116 Surrey Street, Darlinghurst
9332 4052
buffalodiningclub.com.au
Open Wed–Sat 12pm–11pm

- -

As the name suggests, eating at Buffalo Dining Club is all about the cheese. The team import varieties like burrata, caprino and fresh buffalo mozzarella weekly from Italy and pair it with some equally impressive Italian wines. It's that focus on importing fine food and vino that makes visiting here an authentic experience. The small space (spread over two levels), is always buzzing and you might have to lean in to hear your dinner companion. But that just means you get to cosy up to your date … You can people-watch from seats outside if you fancy, or sit by the kitchen and look on as the chefs do their thing.

4.

EDITION COFFEE ROASTERS
265 Liverpool Street, Darlinghurst
editioncoffeeroasters.com
Open Mon–Fri 7am–3.30pm,
Sat–Sun 8am–3.30pm

With concrete floors and blonde wood furniture, Edition Coffee Roasters is a bright and sunny spot at which to start your morning. And it just might be the only place in Sydney where you can get Japanese–Nordic fusion for breakfast. Started by two brothers with an obvious intent on delivering something unique, their international travels have inspired dishes like black rice with coconut yoghurt, fruit and seeds, broth of tofu and pear with crushed walnuts and seaweed. But don't worry, the flavours work perfectly together and will definitely get you out of your comfort zone – in the most delicious way possible.

DARLO BAR

306 Liverpool Street, Darlinghurst
9331 3672
darlobar.com.au
Open Mon–Sun,
10am–midnight

Darlo Bar is a portal between two different worlds – in a good way. The ground floor is like a 1950s living room, decked out with retro posters, pool tables, a few old pinball machines (and some equally mature locals). Take a wander up the stairs, though, and you'll find yourself in a contemporary open-air beer garden, filled with colourful furniture and an equally colourful crowd. With craft beer on tap and a bacon tequila on offer, this portal is your ticket to a good time.

HOT TIP

Order some food here. They bring Thai dishes, burgers and pizza from neighbouring restaurants so It's a good opportunity to support local.

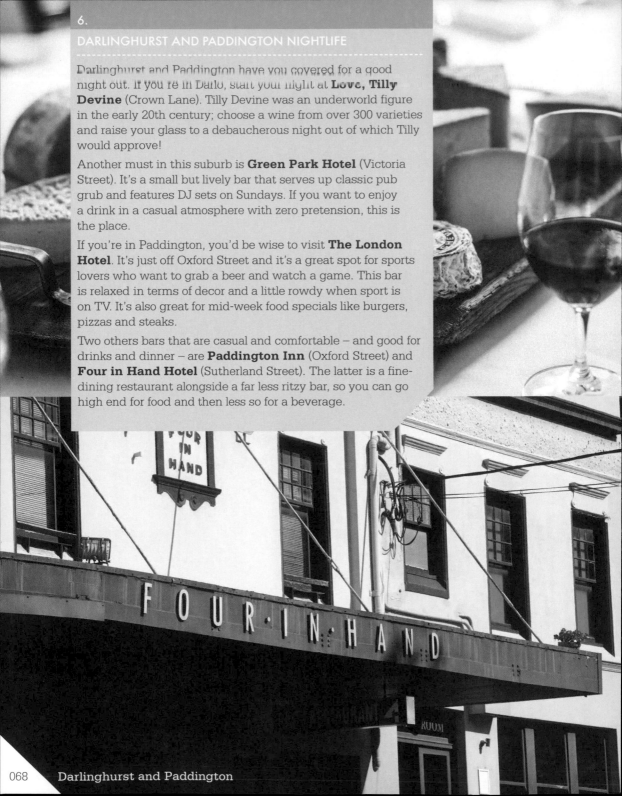

6.

DARLINGHURST AND PADDINGTON NIGHTLIFE

Darlinghurst and Paddington have you covered for a good night out. If you're in Darlo, start your night at **Love, Tilly Devine** (Crown Lane). Tilly Devine was an underworld figure in the early 20th century; choose a wine from over 300 varieties and raise your glass to a debaucherous night out of which Tilly would approve!

Another must in this suburb is **Green Park Hotel** (Victoria Street). It's a small but lively bar that serves up classic pub grub and features DJ sets on Sundays. If you want to enjoy a drink in a casual atmosphere with zero pretension, this is the place.

If you're in Paddington, you'd be wise to visit **The London Hotel**. It's just off Oxford Street and it's a great spot for sports lovers who want to grab a beer and watch a game. This bar is relaxed in terms of decor and a little rowdy when sport is on TV. It's also great for mid-week food specials like burgers, pizzas and steaks.

Two others bars that are casual and comfortable – and good for drinks and dinner – are **Paddington Inn** (Oxford Street) and **Four in Hand Hotel** (Sutherland Street). The latter is a fine-dining restaurant alongside a far less ritzy bar, so you can go high end for food and then less so for a beverage.

7.

PRINT ROOM

11 Glenmore Road, Paddington
0424 034 020
printroom.net.au
Open Wed–Fri 3pm–late,
Sat 12pm–11pm,
Sun 12pm–10pm

It's so nice to experience a bit of dapper, old-world charm in the heart of Sydney's eastern suburbs and the Print Room delivers it. Although the menu is packed with bar snacks, divine share boards (bring on the cheese) and larger plates with a Euro influence, it's the blend of killer cocktails and decor that put this bar at the top of the must-do list. Go for the padded leather booths, marble tabletops, aged mirrors – and the whiskey cocktail, of course.

Tim Duggan knows what's hip and happening in Sydney. As the Content Director of Sound Alliance, he's the mastermind behind popular websites like Junkee, In The Mix and Same Same. With his finger on the pulse of the cool kids, he's definitely a go-to guide on where one should eat, shop and play in these areas.

What's your foolproof breakfast venue?

Just around the corner from my house is Edition (*see* page 066), a cosy Japanese–Nordic fusion breakfast joint, with no eggs or avocados in sight. Instead, it's salmon on pumpernickel, black rice with coconut yoghurt, or berries with rhubarb.

Where do you head for happy hour?

There's a secret back lane hidden behind William Street in the back streets of Darlinghurst that house two of my favourite places to drink; Love, Tilly Devine (*see* page 068) and Red Lily.

Best place to spend an afternoon?

There's no better place to spend a long Sunday lunch than the cosy back room of one of Sydney's first – and finest – gastropubs, the Four in Hand (*see* page 068). It's simple, comfortable and never lets you down.

Any fab stores in the area worth exploring?

My weakness is popping into Incu clothing in Paddington and trying on their well curated range of shirts, jumpers and jackets.

Where do you go to escape the noise of the city?

My parents have a farm about an hour and a half south of Sydney in the Southern Highlands. There's green hills as far as the eye can see, loads of amazing cool-climate wineries like Artemis and Banjo's Run in Exeter and hours of antiquing at places like Hunters & Collectors.

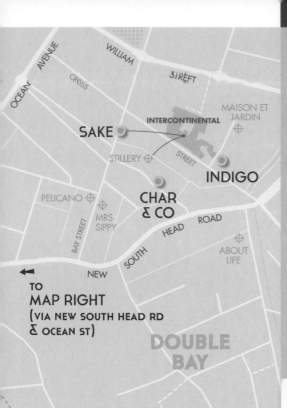

Double Bay and Woollahra are pristine. The streets are lined with trees, the Victorian-era architecture looks lovingly immaculate, and then there's the water in Double Bay. As you wander down Ocean Avenue or Bay Street towards the harbour you'll soon realise why the housing prices are so steep. The views here are second to none.

Woollahra is a suburb back from the water, but its sandstone buildings, quaint cottages and community vibe make it a worthy supporting player.

The people in both suburbs are lovely, with locals who have lived there all their lives. With everything at your doorstep and enough decadent venues to eat, drink and shop in, it's a community you want to be a part of, even if just for a day.

24   JUN 8016

SHOP
1 Queen Street Shopping
2 Terrace
EAT
3 Ladurée

17

EAT AND DRINK
4 Char & Co
5 Chiswick
6 Indigo
7 Saké

DOUBLE BAY
AND WOOLLAHRA

TO CHAR & CO,
SAKE & INDIGO
(SEE MAP LEFT)

N

0   200 m

Trumper Park

HARGRAVE

STREET

JERSEY

OCEAN

ROAD

TRELAWNEY STREET

STREET

PADDINGTON

CHISWICK

Moncur Reserve

MJ BALE

WOOLLAHRA

MONCUR

HERRINGBONE

VICTOR
CHURCHILL

STREET

PARTERRE

STREET

AKIRA

QUEEN

NAPOLEON
PERDIS

LADURÉE

OCEAN STREET

MOORE
PARK
ROAD

TERRACE

MONCUR

ROAD

OXFORD

STREET

STREET

LANG

Centennial Park

*Belvedere
Amphitheatre*

ROAD

*Cannon
Triangle*

CENTENNIAL PARK

YORK

1.

QUEEN STREET SHOPPING

There's big money in Woollahra and the locals are spending it on Queen Street. It's the fashion capital precinct, with designer clothing labels like **Akira** and **Nicola Finetti** for women and **MJ Bale** for men.

Guys and gals who like to dress dapper will lap up the **Herringbone** store; it's got a lot of variety (suits, dresses, skirts, smart jackets), all with that classic, distinguished style Herringbone is known for. When it comes to big names in fashion, you can't pass up the **Napoleon Perdis** lifestyle store, which is just as good for art, jewellery and dinnerware as it is for ready-to-wear clothing.

Lovers of decor and furniture will find their sweet spot in **Parterre**. It's an enchanting French ornate wonderland good for hours of browsing. And if you want to ooh and ahh at the most amazing gourmet butcher in the country, you have to take a peek at **Victor Churchill**. It's like an art gallery inside and is a meat mecca.

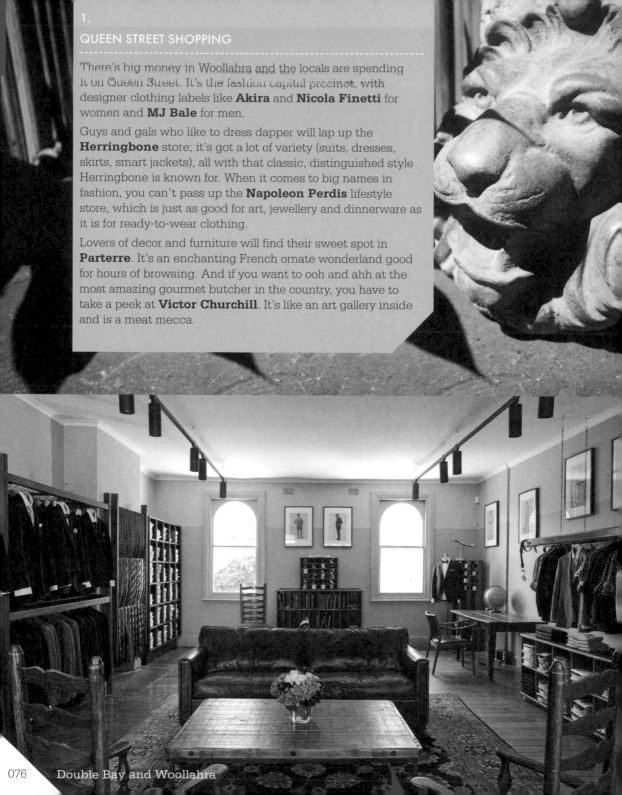

2.

TERRACE
47 Queen Street, Woollahra
9362 5196
terraceoutdoorliving.com.au
Open Mon–Sat 10am–5pm,
Sun 11am–4pm

Everyone in Sydney (or at least the Eastern Suburbs) knows Terrace. It's the colourful beacon of Queen Street and a destination for all things outdoors. Friends Paul Joseph Hopper and Bianca Moore are the creative duo behind the retail store and have a combined background in horticulture, fashion and styling (and their experience in the on-trend store). And it's not all plants and furniture, either. Expect to find a loot of suitcase-friendly goodies like pots, candles, mats, macramé hangers, glassware, fabric and more.

HOT TIP
After some nostril nirvana? Head into Ecoya across the road where scented candles are the name of the game!

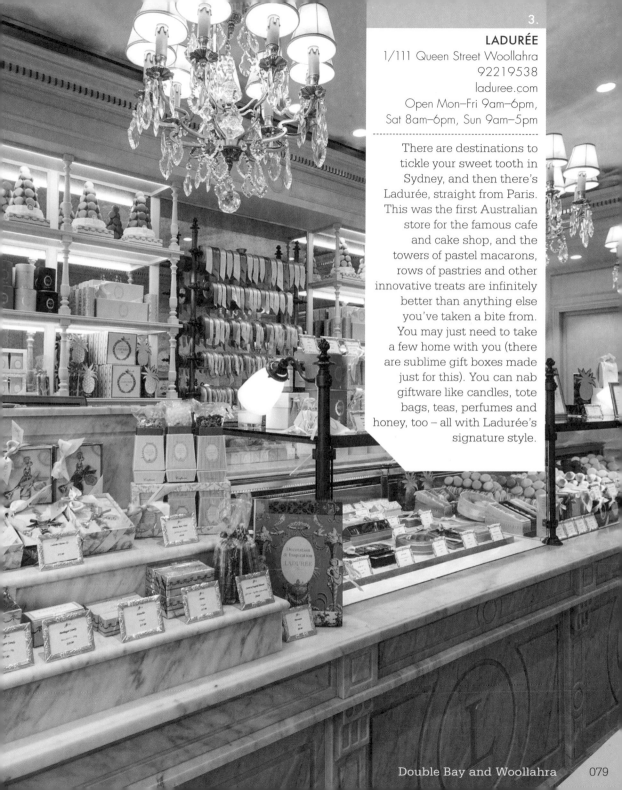

LADURÉE
1/111 Queen Street Woollahra
92219538
laduree.com
Open Mon–Fri 9am–6pm,
Sat 8am–6pm, Sun 9am–5pm

- -

There are destinations to tickle your sweet tooth in Sydney, and then there's Ladurée, straight from Paris. This was the first Australian store for the famous cafe and cake shop, and the towers of pastel macarons, rows of pastries and other innovative treats are infinitely better than anything else you've taken a bite from. You may just need to take a few home with you (there are sublime gift boxes made just for this). You can nab giftware like candles, tote bags, teas, perfumes and honey, too – all with Ladurée's signature style.

4.

CHAR & CO

15 Knox Street, Double Bay
9328 5542
charandco.com.au
Open Tues–Thurs 6pm–midnight,
Friday 12pm–midnight

There's a sense of warmth coming from Char & Co and it's not just from the rotisserie of meats that's constantly turning. Everyone's having a good time here, and while the food is fiery, the restaurant is laid-back and relaxed, with modern-rustic decor and just the right amount of indoor greenery. It's all inspired by Southern Brazil and the locals are lapping it up. Churrasco is by far the most popular choice, teamed with a range of specialty cocktails. It's perfect for a date or a larger group. It's pretty perfect all round, come to think of it.

5.

CHISWICK
65 Ocean Street, Woollahra
8388 8688
chiswickrestaurant.com.au
Open Mon–Thurs 12–2.30pm
& 6–10pm, Fri–Sun 12–3pm,
Fri–Sat 5.30pm–10pm,
Sun 6–10pm

Co-owned by celebrity chef Matt Moran and Peter Sullivan, Chiswick manages to be both approachable and upmarket. Although the restaurant's communal dining table is alluring, go alfresco if you can. You can listen to the calming trickle of the water fountain, take in views of the lush and leafy grounds and nosh on some rather tasty modern-Australian fare. The well-balanced menu is predominantly meat and fish, accompanied by produce that's been hand-picked straight from the kitchen garden. It doesn't get more paddock to plate than this. And never fear if you can't secure a seat outside; almost every table is by a window, so you'll still get an ambient vantage point. There is another Chiswick at the Art Gallery of NSW.

6.

INDIGO

6/15 Cross Street, Double Bay
9363 5966
indigodoublebay.com
Open Mon–Sat 7am–4pm,
Sun 8am–4pm

It's safe to say that life moves a little slower in Double Bay, especially on a lazy Sunday morning. This is when the time is ripe to visit Indigo, as this cafe is at its best on the weekend (although it's easier to nab a table any other day of the week). The crowd is chilled, and the sumptuous breakfast menu contains classic eats but with gourmet, unexpected extras (try the Sri Lankan vegetable-spiced baked eggs or the crunch cornflake French toast). Dine alfresco among the greenery out front – with the sunlight dappling across your coffee, you'll want to stay all day.

HOT T
After some post-brun
shopping? Papier D'Amo
is just across the road ar
is packed to the rafte
with stunning stationer

SAKÉ

The Intercontinental Hotel
33 Cross Street, Double Bay
8017 3104
sakerestaurant.com.au
Open Mon–Sat 11am–3pm &
5pm–late, Sun 10.30am–3pm
& 5pm–late

Saké has four venues Australia-wide and landed in Double Bay just over a year ago. It became an overnight sensation and hasn't slowed down since. What's so good about this Japanese restaurant is the dining options; pull up a solo seat at the sushi bar, grab a table with a date, or sink into a booth with friends. You can order off the menu or go for a chef's banquet, which can be tailored to vegetarians and 'no raw' diners. Speaking of food, options like caramelised miso cod, salt & pepper bugtails and brined pork belly skewers are all must-try delights from the ever-changing menu. The decor is also beyond gorgeous. Think concrete floors, marble table tops and bright floral pops.

Mark Beirne is the entertainment producer at *Sunrise*, Channel Seven's popular television breakfast show. When he's not spending his time with stars from across the globe, he's chilling out in his home suburb of Double Bay. Here Mark names the best venues to visit in his area.

Where does a local go for dinner?

Saké (*see* page 083) at Double Bay is an absolute must – and the classic kingfish with jalapenos dish is worth every cent. Saké also has an impressive cocktail list, beautiful wood and marble decor and friendly service.

How about a cheeky cocktail destination?

Mrs Sippy and Pelicano bring the hip young crowds from all over Sydney. If you want something a bit quieter, the Stillery gin bar at the Intercontinental Hotel has the biggest range of gin cocktails I've ever seen.

Best place to grab Sunday brunch?

Every local will tell you to grab breakfast or brunch at Indigo (*see* page 082). You have the option to sit indoors but I'd recommend grabbing a table on the median strip outside.

Any stores in the area you love to visit?

About Life has great organic produce. For homewares, Maison Et Jardin (Transvaal Avenue) offers gorgeous French provincial pieces at affordable prices.

Where do you go to escape Sydney?

Leura. Beautiful antique homewares shops, gorgeous little cafes and restaurants and scenery that helps free the mind from the hustle and bustle of the city!

Don't feel bad for Enmore, Marrickville or St Peters. While many assume these pockets of the Inner West aren't as interesting as Newtown or Glebe, locals know better. This suburban trio are skilled in putting on a good day and an even better night, with cafes, bars and one-of-a-kind stores.

The Enmore Theatre is one of the main drawcards – bringing people from both near and far to see its shows. Everything around it is pretty amazing, too, so get on foot and go for a wander. It's hard not to get hooked on the local haunts.

MARRICKVILLE

SYDENHAM

Henson Park

ROAD

ROAD

MARRICKVILLE

COFFEE, TEA & ME

ILLAWARRA

MARRICKVILLE ROAD

MARRICKVILLE

VICTORIA ROAD

TO MAP RIGHT (VIA VICTORIA & ENMORE RDS)

CORNERSMITH

MARRICKVILLE

ROAD

Fraser Park

ENMORE, MARRICKVILLE AND ST PETERS

TEMPE

PRINCES HIGHWAY

Cooks River

24   JUN 8016

SHOP
1 Collectika
2 The Society Inc

17

EAT
3 Coffee, Tea and Me
4 Cornersmith
5 West Juliett
EAT AND DRINK
6 Bauhaus West
7 Hartsyard

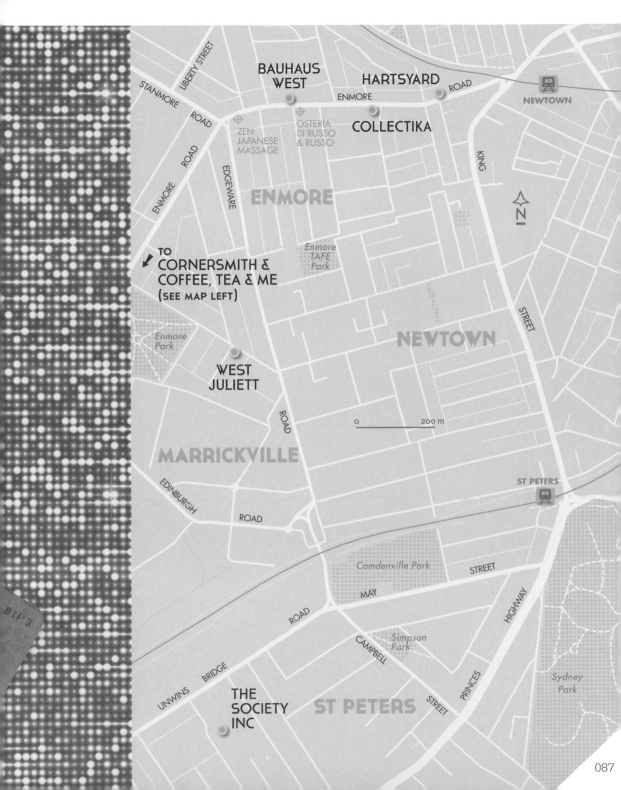

LIBERTY STREET

STANMORE ROAD

ENMORE ROAD

EDGEWARE ROAD

BAUHAUS WEST

HARTSYARD ROAD

ENMORE

NEWTOWN

ZEN JAPANESE MASSAGE

OSTERIA DI RUSSO & RUSSO

COLLECTIKA

ENMORE

KING STREET

N

Enmore TAFE Park

TO CORNERSMITH & COFFEE, TEA & ME (SEE MAP LEFT)

NEWTOWN

Enmore Park

WEST JULIETT

ROAD

0   200 m

MARRICKVILLE

EDINBURGH ROAD

ST PETERS

Camdenville Park

STREET

MAY ROAD

Simpson Park

CAMPBELL

UNWINS BRIDGE

THE SOCIETY INC

ST PETERS

STREET

PRINCES HIGHWAY

Sydney Park

1.

COLLECTIKA

Shop 2, 82–84 Enmore Road, Enmore
9557 8008
collectika.com.au
Open Wed 11am–6pm, Thurs 11am–8pm, Fri 11am–6pm, Sat–Sun 10am–6pm

---

There's a tonne of retro, second-hand furniture stores in Sydney's Inner West. And then there's Collectika. A few minutes in this shop is all it takes to realise the difference. What makes this store stand out is the quality and rarity of the pieces on sale. This isn't salvage yard chic; it's high-end designer pieces your grandmother would have never thrown away. And there's far more on offer than just furniture. Towards the back of the store you can get lost among vinyl records, art and design books, cushions, vintage music players and even some naughty erotic literature. Expect the unexpected here.

2.

THE SOCIETY INC

Warehouse 3.02 75 Mary Street, St Peters
0331 1502
thesocietyinc.com.au
Open Mon–Sat 10am–4pm

It's really hard not to fall in love with stylist and author Sibella Court's design store. Even as you approach the warehouse she set up in 2014 in St Peters, you'll find yourself swept away by its effortless beauty. Once inside, the adoration begins. This is a destination for lovers of homewares, haberdashery, furniture and a host of other curiosities – all with a rustic, boho and seaside edge. Surfboards sit alongside scissors, scullery brushes next to bedding and everything else randomly and wonderfully awaiting your gaze. You won't find anything else like it in Sydney, which is why travelling to find it is worth the effort.

HOT TIP
Park your car on Mary Street and walk through the industrial complex to find The Society Inc's semi-hidden warehouse.

3.

COFFEE, TEA AND ME
100B Sydenham Road,
Marrickville
7900 8045
coffeeteaandme.com.au
Open Mon–Sun 6am–6pm

It's a bit of a blink-and-you'll-miss-it spot, so keep your eyes open as this cosy cafe is well worth popping into for a snack and a sip. Small in size but big in its offering, you'll see sweet treats adorning the counter as you walk in the door; decadent cakes sit beside mouth-watering muffins and charming little cookies that are just made for dunking in tea. The coffee machine is always cranking and there's plenty to look at in the store as you wait for your coffee or tea. The design is nothing fancy, but sometimes the simplest things in life are the best – and that's exactly why you come to this humble coffee house.

CORNERSMITH

314 Illawarra Road, Marrickville
8065 2204
cornersmith.com.au
Open Mon–Thurs 6.30am–
3.30pm, Fri 6.30am–11.30pm,
Sat–Sun 7.30am–3.30pm

Cornersmith is run by a husband and wife team who clearly have a passion for food. Inside this bustling cafe the focus is on honesty and simplicity. The kitchen can be seen from your seat – so it's full transparency all round – and there are a lot of intriguing menu items to sink your teeth into, like smoked mussels, smoky biodynamic brisket and a divine blood orange and sour cream cake. You can also buy and take home pickles and relishes. To help you practise what they preach, Cornersmith holds workshops on everything from preserving to fermenting to cheese making. It's all systems go here and Marrickville is all the better for it.

5.

WEST JULIETT

30 Llewellyn Street, Marrickville
9519 0101
Open Mon–Sun 7am–4pm

It's a good sign when a cafe's always busy. Even better when it has its own merchandise. With both of those things going for it, West Juliett still has a modest, unpretentious and friendly vibe. Its menu is traditional with a twist (expect your eggs to come with braised lentils), while the decor is sleek and simple so as to not overpower the food: concrete floors and white walls make the space feel clean and uncluttered. The crowd is a mix of cool kids and actual kids (you'll find plenty of mums and bubs here and there's space for prams), and, with a range of homemade spreads you can take home with you, it's like this cafe can do no wrong.

6.

BAUHAUS WEST

163 Enmore Road, Enmore
9557 7543
bauhausw.com
Open Wed–Fri 5pm–midnight,
Sat–Sun 12pm–midnight

It's so exciting when a new night-out venue hits Enmore, and Bauhaus West has made quite the impression since its 2014 debut. It's a relaxed place, with its east-meets-west food fusion and laid-back, industrial fit-out doing all the work. The bar tables inside make this an easy place to kick back for a share meal with friends, while the beer garden out back affords you a moodier moment when the sun goes down. The food oozes heart and soul, with mouth-watering crispy pork belly, lobster tail and beef short ribs all possibilities. The cocktail menu is just as amazing (you can't pass up the espresso martini).

HOT TIP

Check out the iconic Enmore Theatre across the road from Bauhaus. It comes alive when there's a show on!

5.

5.

6.

7.

HARTSYARD
33 Enmore Road, Newtown
0068 1473
hartsyard.com.au
Wed–Sun 5.30pm–late

It's certainly not a hole in the wall, but there's something so wonderfully unassuming about the undeniable star of Enmore Road, Hartsyard. This restaurant has a quiet confidence that sees locals lining up to get in from the moment the door swings open, and the fit-out inside is dark and industrial, with exposed pipes and rustic tables. The menu of shared plates is birthed from a nose-to-tail approach to cooking and the produce comes from Hartsyard's very own garden. There are some really interesting selections here, like chicken skin with togarashi, and lime and crispy pigtails with buttermilk dressing. It all makes for a very indulgent evening.

You'll find Enmore local Andrei Meintjes in his store, Collectika, most days of the week. But when it comes time to shut up shop, he's out and about taking in the best the Inner West has to offer.

What are the people like here?

An eclectic, multicultural mix of young families, hipsters, wannabe hipsters, Eastern Suburbs expatriates, creative types, millionaires; just your Licorice All Sorts, really.

Best place for coffee and cake?

West Juliett (*see* page 092) in Marrickville – the coffee is great and their dessert cabinet is to die for. Their banana cake with caramel icing and almonds is deliciously evil.

Foolproof dinner destination?

Osteria di Russo and Russo in Enmore is an absolute no-brainer for dinner. These guys serve up some of the most considered, highly developed, nod to Italian food going around. We feel lucky to have these guys in the hood and dine there when we can.

Winding down.

Zen Japanese massage at the top of Enmore Road is always good for an end-of-week massage. If you head in there most Sundays at around 6pm and hear snoring, you will know that Collectika is in da house.

Escaping the city.

For a quick getaway outside of Sydney, we love Pearl Beach (a 90-minute drive north of Sydney). There are some amazing beach houses available right on the beach. Spend a weekend there and you'll feel like you've been away for a week.

There's a warm sense of community in these three suburbs. On the two main streets – Glebe Point Road and Norton Street – foot traffic is heavy and so are the cars. It's the kind of area you can happily explore on foot though, with loads of historic buildings to check out and diverse stores, cafes and bars.

Because there are two universities here, there's a young crowd eager to enjoy the bustling nightlife of Glebe and Leichhardt (Annandale less so). But these suburbs are also packed with families and an older generation who have been there for years. These suburbs are a little bohemian and if you want to tap into that vibe take a walk to Victoria Park on the corner of Parramatta Road and King Street.

SHOP
1 Glebe Markets
2 The Works
EAT
3 Booth Street Bistro
4 The Wedge Espresso

EAT AND DRINK
5 The Royal Botanical
DRINK
6 The Different Drummer
7 The Little Guy

GLEBE, ANNANDALE AND LEICHHARDT

Iron Cove

LEICHHARDT PARK AQUATIC CENTRE

Leichhardt Park

Leichhardt Oval

LILYFIELD

ROZELLE

VICTORIA ROAD

DARLING STREET

BALMAIN ROAD

Easton Park

PERRY STREET

0   300 m

LILYFIELD

ROAD

CITY WEST LINK

ROZELLE BAY

LEICHHARDT NORTH

LILYFIELD

ELEMENTS I LOVE

CITY WEST LINK

NORTON STREET

CATHERINE STREET

Whites Creek Valley Park

Cohen Park

ROAD

Pioneers Memorial Park

BALMAIN

MOORE

War Memorial Park

Whites Creek

JOHNSTON STREET

NORTON STREET

ALLEN STREET

STREET

BOOTH STREET BISTRO

LEICHHARDT

BOOTH

THE ROYAL BOTANICAL

LEICHHARDT STREET

STREET

STYLES STREET

TERRIFIC SCIENTIFIC

STREET

MARION STREET

PALACE CINEMA

STREET

BALMAIN ROAD

CATHERINE

ANNANDALE

TO
THE LITTLE GUY,
THE DIFFERENT DRUMMER,
THE WEDGE ESPRESSO,
GLEBE MARKETS
& THE WORKS
(SEE MAP LEFT)
→

PARRAMATTA

ROAD

PETERSHAM

STANMORE

STREET

CRYSTAL

PERCIVAL ROAD

SALISBURY

ROAD

BRIDGE ROAD

Johnstons Creek

O'Dea Reserve

PETERSHAM

1.

GLEBE MARKETS

Glebe Public School
Corner Derby Place and
Glebe Point Road
glebemarkets.com.au
Open 10am–4pm every
Saturday

People swarm from all over Glebe (and beyond) to enjoy the live music, gourmet food and recycled finds of this local icon. These markets are the place to find vintage fashion, old CDs and books, arts and crafts, homewares and more. You name it, someone is selling it. Not only that, but there's the distinct feeling you're discovering an emerging artist before they make it big, which is what makes a wander through so exciting. The sense of community is at its greatest here (stall holders will talk to you about their creations), and it's so easy to get swept up in this bohemian way of life – if only for a day.

2.

THE WORKS
62 Glebe Point Road, Glebe
9660 0606
theworksglebe.com.au
Open Mon–Fri 10am–6pm,
Sat 10am–5.30pm,
Sun 11am–5pm

You'd never know it from the outside, but The Works is gigantic. It's not until you head towards the back of the store and see the staircase that you begin to understand how epic it is. Filled to the brim with old knick knacks, some of the vintage finds here are even a little spooky, like asylum signage that'd take someone with real guts to display at home. Once you enter this vintage treasure trove and start rummaging around, you'll find yourself hooked on the bibs and bobs. They also run regular workshops on topics like edible gardening, French furniture stenciling techniques and coffee making. So think ahead and book yourself in.

ASYLUM
WATT ST ENTRANCE

3.

BOOTH STREET BISTRO

127 Booth Street, Annandale
9660 6652
boothstbistro.com
Open Tues–Fri from 7.30am,
Sat & Sun from 8am,
Tues–Sun 12–3pm & from 6pm

It's hard to find a restaurant like Booth Street Bistro, which exudes a sense of elegance without being stuffy. Not only that, but it offers up a menu with a European twist that'll appeal to a wide range of tastes. From oysters to meat boards, oven-roasted lamb rump to banoffee pie with salted caramel ice cream – it's all delicious. Run by a husband and wife team, the fit-out features booth seating in parts and an alfresco area out front that's just made for dining on warm, summer nights. They even share recipes on their website, so after you head home you can infuse some of their flavour into your own food.

THE WEDGE ESPRESSO
53/55 Glebe Point Road, Glebe
9660 3313
Open Mon–Sat 8am–4pm,
Sun 9am–3pm

Brunch venues in the Inner West don't get better than this one. With an atmosphere that's lively but not chaotic, this is a place you can go to with friends or fly solo. Pull up a stool at the bench and look out the giant open windows to the gritty urban streetscape; this is the spot for people-watching or tapping away on your laptop with caffeine at the ready. Sink your teeth into tasty bites like the BBQ short rib bun or the Texan style slow cooked pulled pork. Locals not only rush to dine in at the cafe – especially on weekends – but the take-away coffee line also gets a workout!

HOT TIP
The Wedge Espresso has an out-of-this-world cold coffee on offer and you need to try it!

5.

THE ROYAL BOTANICAL
156 Norton Street, Leichhardt
9569 2638
theroyalleichhardt.com.au
Open Mon–Sun 12pm–late

The Royal has been a Leichhardt icon since 1886, but thankfully its upstairs bar – the recently refurbished Botanical – is giving it a new lease on life. You'll know the stair-climbing exercise is worth it once you get to the top and discover a bar brimming over with 100 plant varieties. You can sit indoors or out with some pretty captivating views over Leichhardt. The menu is traditional pub grub, but done exceptionally well, and they have a Tiny Tots menu for the little ones.

HOT TIP
They do high tea at the
Royal upon request, so
gather some friends and
give it a go!

6.

THE DIFFERENT DRUMMER
185 Glebe Point Road, Glebe
9552 3106
differentdrummer.com
Open Tues–Wed 4.30pm–late,
Thurs–Sat 4.30pm–2am,
Sun 4.30pm–midnight

A tapas and cocktail bar, The Different Drummer has been a local favourite for an eternity. Set in an early 20th-century building on Glebe's main strip, the interior of this watering hole is relaxed and the staff are too. Go beyond the front bar and you'll find yourself in the poster-clad beer garden. The best seats in the house are in this back area, although once you have one of their signature cocktails in hand (try a spiced pineapple gobbler), it really doesn't matter where you sit and sip. Chargrilled lamb brochettes and pulled pork tacos are just two must-try picks from their menu.

7.

THE LITTLE GUY
87 Glebe Point Road, Glebe
8084 2037
thelittleguy.com.au
Open Mon–Fri 4pm–midnight,
Sat 1pm–midnight,
Sun 3–10pm

The Little Guy is much like the name suggests; it's pretty little on the ground floor. But what it lacks in floor space, it more than makes up for in atmosphere – and the same goes for the drinks list. Specialising in local craft beer, boutique wines and an ever-changing cocktail list, this Glebe favourite is always bustling. They do live music on Tuesday to Thursday and Sunday, plus Monday trivia and some open mic nights. There's an intoxicating community feel here (even if you don't have a tipple), and you're likely to make new friends.

HOT TIP

The Different Drummer happy hour runs from 6–7.30pm and includes discounted cocktails.

Brooke Crowle's store, Elements I Love, is one of Leichhardt's most stunning. When she's not scouring the country for antiques and other treasures to fill it with, Brooke's out and about enjoying the Inner West's best restaurants, cafes and other hangouts.

Where do you go to unwind?

I love Palace Cinema in Norton Street, Leichhardt, for the latest French films; always enjoyable with a glass of rosé in hand.

Best places for shopping?

I love flowers, and I know who to call when I need something special for the showroom: George from Seed Flora – he's the best in the business! A must-visit shop for young folks and the young at heart would be Terrific Scientific, a toy-and-games shop with a difference in Annandale.

Where can we find you at cocktail hour?

The Royal Botanical (*see* page 104) has recently had a refresh and is great for a drink after work. At the top of my list for eating out would be the Glebe Point Diner.

When the sun is shining

Living and working in Leichhardt, the Bay Run is always there to remind me that I should be doing more exercise! It's a good 7 kilometre run, but I prefer to swim at the Leichhardt Park Aquatic Centre a few times a week.

Where do you go to escape the city?

Byron Bay on the North Coast or Bermagui on the South Coast for local getaways. Both are equally beautiful.

THE BOATHOUSE
AT PALM BEACH,
TO
NOT SHOWN ON MAP
(VIA BARRENJOEY RD)

PITTWATER

MONA VALE

ROAD

ROAD

BARRENJOEY

DARLEY

STREET

LITTLE
PAPER
LANE

Kitchener
Park

PITTWATER ROAD

ARMCHAIR
COLLECTIVE

Mona Vale
Golf Club

TO
MAP RIGHT
(VIA PITTWATER RD)

MANLY
AND BEYOND

Surf culture meets urban cool at Manly's iconic beach, home to chilled out locals, surfers and travellers. Many of its cafes and restaurants serve up seaside views, and its shopping streets are laid-back. Manly is the gateway to the Northern Beaches, which epitomise carefree Australian beach living with their village vibes – and beaches.

Get the ferry from the city and make a day of Manly. You can bask in the coastal charm by walking along the beach promenade or chilling out watching the waves at a cafe or bar. It is just as magical at night with the relaxed vibe the locals have created. You'll definitely want to stay a while in this suburb and the ones beyond it – they're all picturesque.

24   JUN 8016

SHOP
1 HONEY BEE HOMEWARES
2 LITTLE PAPER LANE
SHOP AND EAT
3 ARMCHAIR COLLECTIVE

17

EAT
4 PAPI CHULO
5 THE BOATHOUSE AT
  PALM BEACH
EAT AND DRINK
6 DONNY'S BAR & RESTAURANT
7 THE IVANHOE HOTEL

NARRABEEN

PARK PARADE

Warriewood
Beach

Tasman Sea

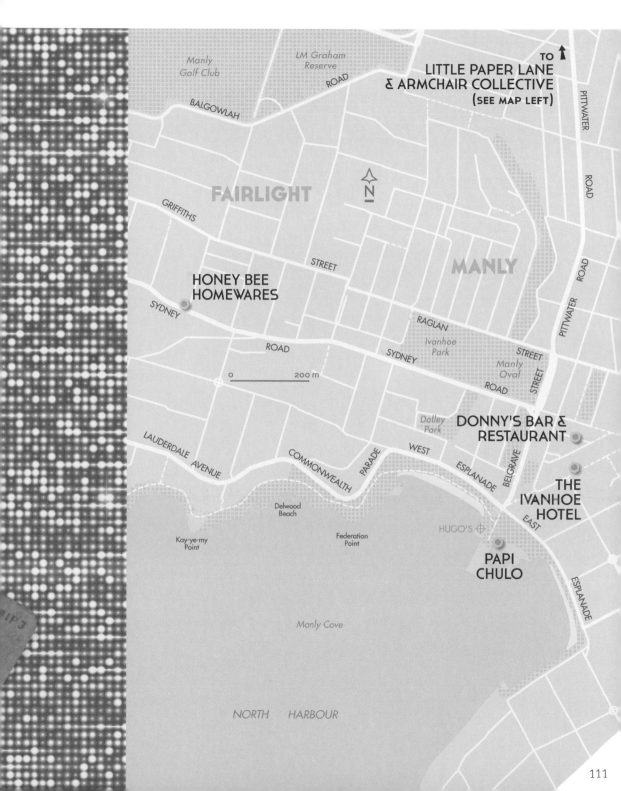

Manly
Golf Club

LM Graham
Reserve

ROAD

TO ↑
LITTLE PAPER LANE
& ARMCHAIR COLLECTIVE
(SEE MAP LEFT)

PITTWATER

ROAD

BALGOWLAH

FAIRLIGHT

N

MANLY

GRIFFITHS

STREET

HONEY BEE
HOMEWARES

RAGLAN

Ivanhoe
Park

SYDNEY

PITTWATER

SYDNEY

STREET

ROAD

Manly
Oval

STREET

0   200 m

ROAD

Dalley
Park

DONNY'S BAR &
RESTAURANT

LAUDERDALE

AVENUE

COMMONWEALTH

PARADE

WEST

ESPLANADE

BELGRAVE

THE
IVANHOE
HOTEL

Delwood
Beach

EAST

Federation
Point

HUGO'S ✛

Kay-ye-my
Point

PAPI
CHULO

ESPLANADE

Manly Cove

NORTH   HARBOUR

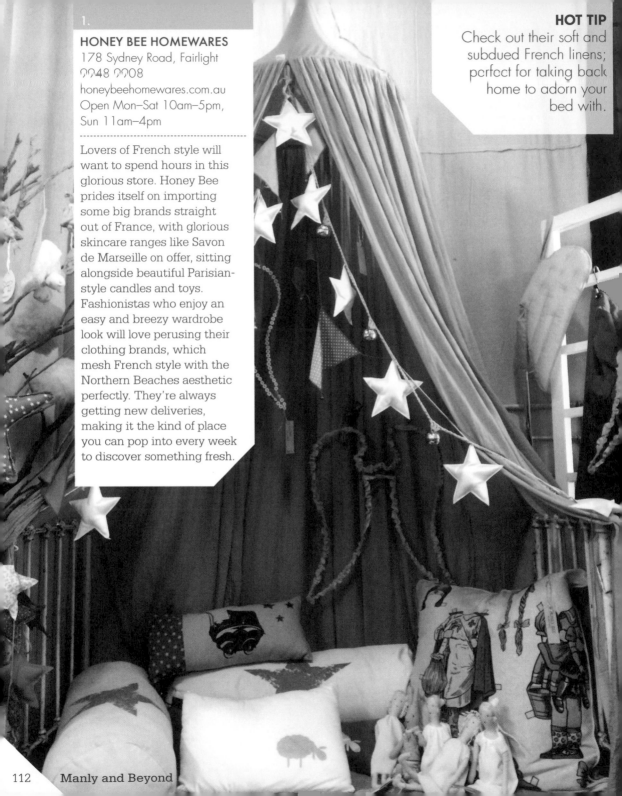

1.

HONEY BEE HOMEWARES
178 Sydney Road, Fairlight
9948 9908
honeybeehomewares.com.au
Open Mon–Sat 10am–5pm,
Sun 11am–4pm

Lovers of French style will want to spend hours in this glorious store. Honey Bee prides itself on importing some big brands straight out of France, with glorious skincare ranges like Savon de Marseille on offer, sitting alongside beautiful Parisian-style candles and toys. Fashionistas who enjoy an easy and breezy wardrobe look will love perusing their clothing brands, which mesh French style with the Northern Beaches aesthetic perfectly. They're always getting new deliveries, making it the kind of place you can pop into every week to discover something fresh.

HOT TIP
Check out their soft and subdued French linens; perfect for taking back home to adorn your bed with.

LITTLE PAPER LANE

Shop 5/1 Waratah Street,
Mona Vale
8407 9204
littlepaperlane.com.au
Open Mon–Fri 10am–5.30pm,
Sat 10am–4pm

So it's a little while out of Manly (30 minutes along Pittwater Road), but Little Paper Lane is a stationery haven you simply have to visit. Run by Jayde Leeder and husband Steve, their front window displays are so popular they have their own Instagram hashtag and people flock to the store to see what merchandising magic this duo create – especially at Christmas. The loot you'll find inside is both imported from overseas and sourced locally, with some products created in-house. It's all super-affordable too, so you can grab a stack of presents for friends and family, along with some treasures for yourself.

HOT TIP

There's a great spot right beside Little Paper Lane called MX, serving up killer Mexican food you can devour for lunch.

3.

ARMCHAIR COLLECTIVE

9 Darley Street, Mona Vale

9999 2871

thearmchair.com.au

Open Mon–Sun 7am–4pm

It seems there is nothing Armchair Collective can't do. It's a cafe, it's a home-and-lifestyle store and they also run an interior design service and furniture re-upholstery. For lovers of a sip and a spend, you can't go past it. There are also cushions and custom lampshades up for grabs, so you're bound to walk out with something for your home. Oh, and did I mention it's a 50 metre walk to Mona Vale beach? There's nothing else like it in Sydney.

PAPI CHULO

22–23 Manly Wharf, Manly
9240 3000
merivale.com.au/papichulo
Open Mon–Fri 12–10.30pm,
Sat 11.30am–10.30pm,
Sun 11.30am–9pm

Take everything you know about a traditional Aussie barbecue and throw it out the window. Papi Chulo is a serious smokehouse with American Deep South influences. Think marinated meats six hours in the making, infused with flavour and paired with side dishes that taste just as international. Ranger's Valley wagyu brisket and Suffolk lamb ribs with Papi's BBQ sauce are two standouts, not to mention the smoked hot wings (the comeback sauce is utterly divine). This is smokehouse decor done Manly style – it's contemporary and colourful, and more beachy than brooding, and with a location smack bang on the waterfront (ideal to eat at before your ferry to the city comes in), this seaside diner is a hard one to pass up.

THE BOATHOUSE AT PALM BEACH

Barronjoey Boathouse, Governor
Phillip Park, Palm Beach
9974 5440
theboathousepb.com.au
Open Mon–Sun 7am–4pm

You'll gasp in a gulp of that fresh Pittwater air upon entering The Boathouse in Palm Beach, where the rich and famous holiday and the iconic Australian television series, *Home and Away*, is filmed. Everything about the Boathouse is picturesque, and feels like you're in a scene from a movie (the decor is casual and rustic but super, super charming). There's seating both inside and out, but you'd be hard-pressed to find someone who wouldn't want to enjoy an alfresco breakfast and take in the view over Pittwater out to Ku-ring-gai Chase. The Boathouse also serves up a delectable lunch, which is predominantly seafood inspired. But food aside, the views alone are worth the drive up to Palm Beach. Make sure you take a camera (and your appetite).

6.

DONNY'S BAR & RESTAURANT

7 Market Lane, Manly
9977 1887
donnys.com.au
Open Mon–Thurs 4pm–late,
Fri 4pm–midnight,
Sat 12pm–midnight,
Sun 12pm–10pm

If any venue could be described as a dapper New York loft outside of the Big Apple, it's Donny's. The juxtaposition this bar and restaurant presents is refreshing, as it's the last kind of design aesthetic you'd expect to find in a seaside suburb. Once you've lost your mind over the industrial lights, exposed brick and worn leather armchairs, grab a menu. It's also rather unexpected, with gourmet pub grub, Asian dumplings and seafood on offer. And the boutique beers aren't half bad, either.

THE IVANHOE HOTEL
27 The Corso, Manly
9976 3955
ivanhoehotelmanly.com.au
Open Mon–Sun 11.30am–late

The Ivanhoe's heritage facade stands out among the Aussie flag t-shirt shops and ice-cream parlours of Manly's pedestrian mall, the Corso. As you walk through the heavy timber doors and into the best interior in Manly, the Hampton's vibe sets the scene for a relaxed, beachy afternoon (with classic pub food). The many indoor and outdoor spaces mean you're spoilt for choice as to where to sit and soak up the atmosphere. It might not be right on the beach, but with design this good, it's close enough.

Sonia Stackhouse is the talented lady behind lifestyle blog Life, Love and Hiccups. The mum of three is a Northern Beaches local who frequents the venues in this chapter for a bite, bevvie and bit of 'me time'.

What's the community like here?

The vibe on the Northern Beaches could be described as laid-back, casual-hip. The wider community among the stores and businesses has a tight-knit camaraderie that you don't often see these days.

Best cafe in the area?

The Pelican Pavilion right on Collaroy Beach. Grab yourself a table and do not move. I have a habit of arriving in the morning with my laptop and working my way (literally and figuratively) through the menu whilst I sort of kind of pretend to work.

Where will we find you at cocktail hour?

I don't think you can go past Hugo's at Manly Wharf for a cocktail with a perfect view.

Best places to shop?

Avalon is the place to shop on the Northern Beaches. You can't not go to Table Tonic, Rust, Beachwood and Bookoccino. If you're heading to Avalon, you must stop at Little Paper Lane (*see* page 113) in Mona Vale.

Where do you escape to?

Byron Bay – it's our home away from home, but is different enough to still give me that fabulously giddy holiday buzz.

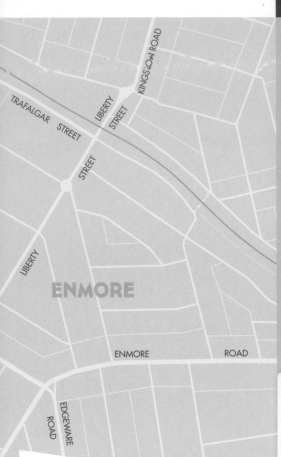

ENMORE

TRAFALGAR STREET
LIBERTY STREET
KINGSTON ROAD
STREET
LIBERTY
ENMORE ROAD
EDGEWARE ROAD

NEWTOWN
AND ERSKINEVILLE

EDGEWARE ROAD
NEWTOWN

If you're looking to explore suburbs with an anything-goes vibe, Newtown and Erskineville are it. While both are filled with colourful characters, Newtown is undoubtedly the more entertaining of the two. King Street is one of the most diverse streets in Sydney when it comes to shopping. Sticking to it is the best way to discover the must-see shops – and locals – in Newtown. Erskineville has more of a village feel and both suburbs are filled with gorgeous Victorian and Edwardian terraces.

There are no water views but the busy streets, independent stores and numerous watering holes are what makes these Inner West suburbs so awesome. And the locals, of course.

24   JUN 8976

SHOP
1 King Street Shopping
2 T Totaler
EAT
3 Brewtown Newtown

17

EAT AND DRINK
4 Earl's Juke Joint
5 Rose of Australia
DRINK
6 Corridor
7 Miss Peaches

MISS
PEACHES

CORRIDOR

BREWTOWN
NEWTOWN

MISSENDEN ROAD

STREET

WATKIN

AUSTRALIA

STREET

Camperdown
Memorial
Rest Park

MONSTER
THREADS

STREET

STREET

BLUE DOG
PRINTS &
POSTERS

MARYS

OCTOPUS
DESIGN

BOYLAN
HEADWEAR

KING

WILSON

ERSKINEVILLE

ENMORE   ROAD

KING   STREET

NEWTOWN

NEWTOWN

ROAD

CHARLES   STREET

EARL'S
JUKE
JOINT

BLOODWOOD

FLEETWOOD
MACCHIATO

ROSE OF
AUSTRALIA

REPRESSED
RECORDS

ERSKINEVILLE

ERSKINEVILLE

KING

N

0   100 m

STREET

T TOTALER

KING STREET SHOPPING

King Street is a true mixed bag of shopping delights. It's all independent retailers and many of the stores are set in old Victorian terraces, which makes shopping on the strip pretty special.

Octopus Design is great for gifts and if you have kids they'll adore a look in this colourful wonderland. It stocks melamine dinnerware for little ones, toys, kitchenware, small decorative items and an entire wall of greeting cards, wrapping paper and stationery.

Blue Dog Prints & Posters has super affordable art prints with edge. Think cheeky slogans, comic book and action hero imagery, and a lot of abstract art. Many of the pieces are small enough to roll up and pack in a suitcase.

Monster Threads is a cool fashion hub selling quirky tees, shirts, jackets and other pieces for both genders. They also have a unique jewellery counter, with wooden brooches and other one-of-a-kind adornments.

Down the St Peters end of King Street, you'll find **Repressed Records**. It's a great visit for lovers of vintage tunes but they stock an array of cool tees as well.

2.

T TOTALER
555A King Street, Newtown
0466 136 302
ttotalertea.com
Open Wed–Fri 11am–5pm,
Sat–Sun 10am–5pm

- -

T Totaler is an artisan loose-leaf-tea company and cafe, located down the St Peters end of King Street. It's a humble fit-out but has plenty of heart. Drop in and grab one of their 30 divine loose-leaf tea varieties to take away. They present them in the cutest amber glass jars and recyclable bags. If you fancy sitting in to enjoy your brew, you can do that too. Speak to the team about their regular tea tasting events. It's here they'll show you how to match their blends and varieties and complement them with delicious cakes.

GROWN TO BE BREWED

EST MMXII

T totaler

№ 3 | Foraging for Berries | 80 g

PERSONALLY PICKED & PACKAGED IN AUSTRALIA

3.

BREWTOWN NEWTOWN

6–8 O'Connell Street, Newtown
8001 1001
brewtownnewtown.com
Open Mon–Sun 8am–4pm

The one exception to the sticking to King Street rule is Brewtown, tucked down O'Connell Street and home to the legendary cronut (a delicious combination of a croissant and a donut). It's not all sweet treats in this cafe, though; the menu is packed with paddock-to-plate dishes for breakfast and lunch. The added bonus: head up the stairs and land in O'Connell Street Merchants – a retail store full of fashion, art and quirky lifestyle products. You should never visit one without seeing the other.

HOT TIP
Look for the 'Betta Meats' sign or you'll completely miss this classic.

4.

EARL'S JUKE JOINT
407 King Street, Newtown
Open Mon–Sat 4pm–midnight,
Sun 4–10pm

From the outside it looks like an abandoned butcher shop, but pass through the doors of Earl's Juke Joint and you'll find yourself in a dark and brooding cocktail bar; one that gives a generous nod to the Deep South while still feeling local. The walls are clad with vintage photos of blues artists, the bar staff are expert in just about any drink of poison you could dream up and the art deco fit-out is just what the decor doctor ordered. They don't serve food, so make this a pre-dinner or post-dessert destination.

ROSE OF AUSTRALIA
1 Swanson Street, Erskineville
9565 1441
roseofaustralia.com
Open Mon 10am–11pm,
Tues–Sat 10am–midnight,
Sun 10am–10pm

Established in 1874, it really doesn't get more historic than this art deco pub – recently freshened up with a makeover in 2015. The venue still retains the family-friendly, working-class vibe it became famous for over a century ago (with a kids' menu and high chairs available for little ones). The team flawlessly meshes that traditional feel with a fresh, contemporary aesthetic – attracting a new generation to mingle with its seasoned clientele. Walk beyond the front bar and you'll find the show-stopper – a bright, industrial beer garden with a wall of lush greenery that'll make even the most discerning green thumbs weak at the knees. The food is traditional pub grub favourites like ribs, burgers, steaks and more.

EAT
DRINK
PLAY

EAT
DRINK
PLAY

OUR PHILOSOPHY
NO ROOM HIRE
NO MINIMUM SPEND
NO HIDDEN EXTRAS

OUR SPACES
THE STANDARD

6.

CORRIDOR

153A King Street, Newtown
0422 873 879
corridorbar.com.au
Open Tue–Fri 3pm–midnight,
Sat 1pm–midnight,
Sun 1–10pm

The name says a lot about
the way this venue looks and
feels; it's a dark and narrow
local haunt set up in an old
terrace house. The bottom
floor of Corridor houses its
only bar along with a few
cosy spots to sit. There's an
indoor section on its first
floor, but it's upstairs in the
beer garden where most of
the action happens, so have
your elbows ready to fight for
a seat. The entire set-up is, in
true Newtown style, laid-back
and anything goes. The menu
is possibly the best part, with
an unbeatable share board –
you'll battle to get through
the portion (think cheese,
antipasto, calamari, chicken
and more). Beer, wine and
cocktails are all top-notch too.

7.

MISS PEACHES

201 Missenden Road, Newtown
9557 7280
misspeaches.com.au
Open Wed–Sun 5pm–midnight

Even the most unfit among
us will be willing to climb
the windy stairs to reach the
top of this culinary castle.
Situated above the ever-
popular Marlborough Hotel,
Miss Peaches is worlds
apart from the bar beneath
it. Hands-down the best
soul food kitchen in Sydney,
its lively atmosphere, killer
cocktail list and range of
indulgent fare will make
this destination an instant
favourite. The vibe inside
is a little rockabilly and a
little swing – with pork
ribs and gumbo dishes to
complement. The range of
share dishes are so sinfully
delicious that you'll count
your blessings you leave via
a downward stair, not an
uphill one.

HOT TIP

Miss Peaches is great
for groups. Book one of
their colourful booths and
sample a bit of everything
from the menu.

Christopher Thé is the director of Black Star Pastry. Everyone in the Inner West knows that his bakery chain is the place to go for all things sweet and delicious. There's one in Newtown, a second in Rosebery and a third at the Powerhouse Museum. With this in mind, I had to ask this creative genius where he likes to eat, drink and shop in the area.

Where do you head for breakfast?

Fleetwood Macchiato in Erskineville. They have a great vibe and keep things interesting.

Best place to grab dinner in the area?

Mary's in Newtown for their burgers and fried chicken. They are addictive and come with a side of remorse at the end.

Where do the cool kids drink?

Bloodwood on King Street in Newtown makes great cocktails.

Where do you go to escape Sydney?

The countryside around the outskirts of Hunter Valley.

There's a charm in the journey from North Sydney to Mosman that you really need to experience. It's affluence without arrogance, quaint, charming and in some pockets, wonderfully historic. Keep your eyes peeled for some pretty impressive yachts on the dazzling harbour.

From the city, walk across the Harbour Bridge (access is via Cumberland Street in The Rocks) and then visit Luna Park, the city's most iconic theme park, on the other side. It's here you'll take in a view of Sydney so breathtaking you won't want to leave.

Once you get out of the North Sydney business district and into Kirribilli with its historic houses and spectacular harbour and bridge views, puff your way through beautiful, hilly Neutral Bay and wind your way towards swanky Mosman.

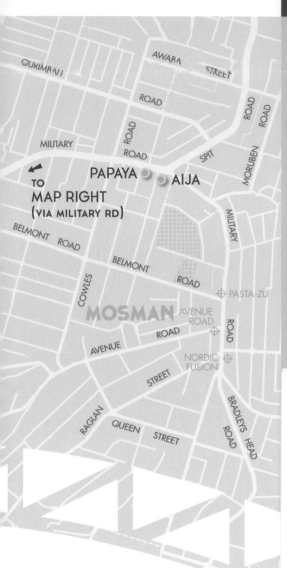

TO
MAP RIGHT
(VIA MILITARY RD)

24   JUN 8076

SHOP
1 Aija
2 Papaya

17

EAT
3 Bourke Street Bakery
EAT AND DRINK
4 The Greens
5 The Oaks
6 The Treehouse Hotel

NORTH SYDNEY
TO MOSMAN

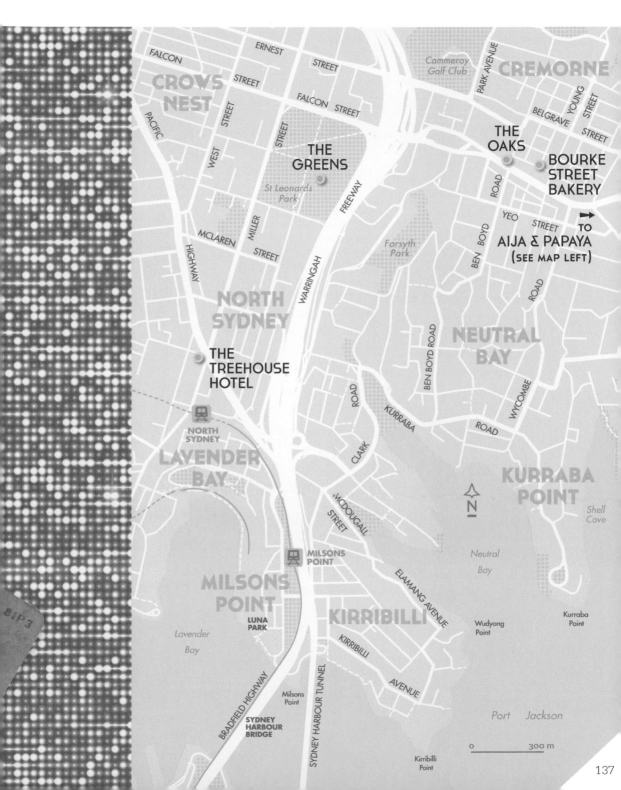

FALCON STREET
ERNEST STREET
Cammeray Golf Club
PARK AVENUE
CREMORNE

CROWS NEST
FALCON STREET
PACIFIC
WEST STREET
STREET
STREET

BELGRAVE STREET
YOUNG STREET
THE OAKS
BOURKE STREET BAKERY
ROAD

THE GREENS
St Leonards Park
FREEWAY
YEO STREET
TO
AIJA & PAPAYA
(SEE MAP LEFT)

MCLAREN
MILLER STREET
HIGHWAY
WARRINGAH
Forsyth Park
BEN BOYD

NORTH SYDNEY
BEN BOYD ROAD
NEUTRAL BAY
ROAD

THE TREEHOUSE HOTEL
ROAD
KURRABA
WYCOMBE ROAD

NORTH SYDNEY
CLARK

LAVENDER BAY
KURRABA
KURRABA POINT
Shell Cove

MCDOUGALL STREET
N

MILSONS POINT
Neutral Bay

MILSONS POINT
ELAMANG AVENUE
Wudyong Point
Kurraba Point

LUNA PARK
KIRRIBILLI

Lavender Bay
KIRRIBILLI
Port Jackson

BRADFIELD HIGHWAY
AVENUE
Milsons Point
SYDNEY HARBOUR BRIDGE
SYDNEY HARBOUR TUNNEL
0   300 m

Kirribilli Point

1.

AIJA
2/559 Military Road, Mosman
9960 2458
aijabrand.com.au
Open Mon–Sat 9am–5pm

It's hard not to get a little excited walking into Aija. The store is sun-drenched and bright, there's a fragrant smell of leather in the air and the products are to die for. This is your go-to store for quality leather handbags and purses, eclectic jewellery pieces, stunning scarves and a few unexpected home decor gems. Run by sisters Maali and Riina, the store's products feel casual but effortlessly chic at the same time, and all have an inherent timeless quality. Be prepared to spend up a storm.

2.

PAPAYA
539 Military Road, Mosman
8571 7799
papaya.com.au
Open Mon–Sun 10am–5pm

Papaya is a subdued homewares paradise, and despite having another location in Bondi Junction, the Mosman store is where their pieces truly shine. Light beams in through their front window onto timber tables, scented candles and a sea of soft furnishings. Step into the courtyard (on to tiles that came from the Opera House forecourt) and witness the beauty of their 18th-century Chinese doors. It's a truly magical moment in this much-loved decor destination.

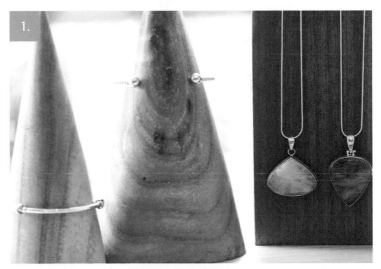

3.

BOURKE STREET BAKERY

Shop 7/19–25 Grosvenor Street,
Neutral Bay
9953 5555
bourkestreetbakery.com.au
Open Mon–Fri 7am–4pm,
Sat–Sun 7am–5pm

Don't be fooled by the name. While the Neutral Bay arm of this bakery is on Grosvenor Street, its flagship store began years ago in Bourke Street in Surry Hills. Potential confusion aside, this is one dine-in or take-out bakery you don't want to miss. Grab a coffee and your fave baked treat and sit outside in the sun. It's a family-friendly haven with kids and grown-ups all mingling and munching away. The locals – like with every Bourke Street Bakery arm – flock in droves to dine here. And, after you experience their pastries, tarts, pies, cookies and cakes, you'll know why.

SAUSAGE ROLLS

pork & fennel $4.50
lamb, harissa & almond $4.50
eggplant, chickpea & feta $4

THE GREENS
50 Ridge Street, North Sydney
9245 3099
thegreensnorthsydney.com.au
Open Sun–Thurs 11.30am–
11pm, Fri–Sat 11.30am–12am

The Greens is the most-bustling place north of the bridge, especially if the sun's out. This is where the younger crowd in North Sydney go to play, with lawn bowls outside and an even cooler interior going on inside thanks to a recent renovation. The menu features small plates, substantial bites and a lot of sides (the goldband snapper, crispy pork belly and wagyu beef burger are all sublime). This is the perfect sip-and-snack venue for the after-work crowd (and weekenders who love a bit of fun in the sun). The kids' menu proves that this isn't just for adults. It's a great spot for the whole family.

HOT TIP
Ask for the Pineapple and Ginger Fizz. This drink serves four and is truly delicious.

5.

THE OAKS

118 Military Road, Neutral Bay
9953 5515
oakshotel.com.au
Open Mon–Thurs 10am–midnight,
Fri–Sat 10am–1.30am,
Sun 12pm–midnight

A few years ago, The Oaks underwent a four-million-dollar revamp and the results are wonderfully obvious. This venue is not only massive but now very on-trend, pulling a crowd of young people who want to dig into their pub grub in glamorous surrounds. The giant oak tree, which sits in the beer garden, drops acorns in autumn, which in local folklore is said to bring luck to those they strike.

HOT TIP
Try this venue at night. The fairy lights that are strewn over the giant tree come on to create a magical moment!

THE TREEHOUSE HOTEL
60 Miller Street, North Sydney
8458 8980
thetreehousehotel.com.au
Open Mon–Fri 7am–late,
Sat 2pm–late

Set among a stack of high-rise buildings, The Treehouse Hotel is a luxe sanctuary, restaurant and bar. From the street, you'd have no idea what awaits you at the top of the stairs. But once you reach the peak, the decadence begins. Treehouse attracts the after-work crowd in North Sydney and comes alive of an evening, when the leafy terrace lights up. Step inside for a seductive vibe that channels a dark *Alice in Wonderland*. The menu is modern Australian, with the lunchtime steak sandwich a clear standout. Pair it with a wine from their impressive list and you're set.

Musician Jack Colwell has spent almost his whole life in Mosman, soaking up the best eateries and hangouts the area has to offer. Although he now lives in the Inner West of Sydney, he's always going over the bridge for work and to see his family.

What's the community like here?

Mosman is pretty low-key. But having said that, there's a lot of life in the suburb during the day. It's great for families and there seems to be a great sense of community at the centre of things.

Any must-do breakfast spots?

I love going to Avenue Road cafe. It's one of the sleeker, cooler spots to visit. The coffee beans provided by Double Roasters (Marrickville brewed) take a little bit of the Inner West and give it to the North Shore.

Where do you love to shop?

Nordic Fusion would be the best and most interesting store in Mosman. A boutique shop for all things Scandinavian. I particularly like their fabric collections; really bold, large graphic prints in eye popping colour.

The best place to go for dinner?

Pasta-Zu has been a longtime favourite of mine. All the pasta is cooked on premise and they offer a wide range of salads and pastas. It also stays open a little later than the other restaurants in Mosman.

Glitz and glamour are more at home in Potts Point, Woolloomooloo and Elizabeth Bay than elsewhere in Sydney. There's money and sophistication in this inner-city precinct, juxtaposed with a raw grittiness that spills over from neighbouring Kings Cross – it makes for an interesting mix of people. Restaurants and bars are plentiful in Woolloomooloo, as are water views. Potts Point and Elizabeth Bay are hubs for shopping, and there are some stellar spots to wine and dine, too.

The Wharf at Woolloomooloo is the most iconic site in this precinct, and the restaurants that run along it are all worthy of exploration.

Map labels: WYNYARD, SYDNEY, STREET, KING, STREET, GEORGE, MARKET, YORK, CLARENCE, ST JAMES, ELIZABETH, Hyde Park, PARK, STREET, TOWN HALL, BATHURST, CROSS CITY TUNNEL, PITT, STREET, Hyde Park, CAMPBELL, Belmore Park, ELIZABETH STREET, SURRY HILLS, STREET, CENTRAL

24 JUN 6076

SHOP
1 Becker Minty
EAT
2 Flour and Stone

EAT AND DRINK
3 Bottega del Vino
4 Gazebo
5 Jimmy Liks
6 Kingsleys Steak and Crabhouse
7 Ms G's
8 Peekaboos

17

POTTS POINT TO WOOLLOOMOOLOO

Royal Botanic Gardens

CAHILL EXPRESSWAY

The Domain

Woolloomooloo Bay

ROADWAY

KINGSLEYS STEAK & CRABHOUSE

ART GALLERY OF NEW SOUTH WALES

COWPER

WHARF

POTTS POINT

STREET

SYDNEY

The Domain

WOOLLOOMOOLOO

BOTTEGA DEL VINO

MACLEAY

BECKER MINTY

FLOUR AND STONE

⊕ RILEY STREET GARAGE

MS. G'S

ROOM 10 ⊕

Fitzroy Gardens

PEEKABOOS

JIMMY LIKS

GAZEBO

ROAD

CROSS CITY TUNNEL

KINGS CROSS

DARLINGHURST

AVENUE

WILLIAM STREET

DISTRIBUTOR

THE GOODWILL SOCIETY ⊕

WARD

CRAIGEND STREET

N

0   200 m

DARLINGHURST ROAD

VICTORIA STREET

DARLINGHURST

EASTERN

Green Park

VICTORIA STREET

BOUNDARY

MCLACHLAN AVENUE

STREET

DARLINGHURST ROAD

147

1.

BECKER MINTY

Shop 7, Ikon Building,
81 Macleay Street, Potts Point
8356 9999
beckerminty.com
Open Mon–Sat 10.30am–6pm,
Sunday 10.30am–5pm

Entering the decadent and
lavish world of Becker Minty
is like being transported to the
Moulin Rouge. Cement floors,
dark walls, leather armchairs
and the most amazing
chandeliers all work to make
this retail hub a sophisticated
shopping experience. If you'd
like to transport the Moulin
Rouge home, the retro (and
sometimes eerie) art, lighting
and furniture on sale will set
the scene. For treasure you
can fit in your suitcase, you'll
fall in love with their vintage
jewellery, retro men's and
women's clothing and some
one-of-a-kind ornaments
(gold skulls and snakes are
the standouts).

FLOUR AND STONE
53 Riley Street, Woolloomooloo
8068 8818
flourandstone.com.au
Open Mon–Fri 7am–4pm,
Sat 8am–4pm

Flour and Stone is worth hunting down in the sea of restaurants in the Darlinghurst end of Woolloomooloo. It's the brainchild of Nadine Ingram, whose experience at a number of other successful establishments led her to create this bakery. It's filled with nostalgic treats made with an authenticity you don't see much of these days. Cakes, slabs and cookies are all phenomenally tasty, but make sure you also try the savoury selection (the slow-braised lamb pie is a winner). Pair those delectable eats with amazing coffee and this might just be your Sydney favourite.

3.

BOTTEGA DEL VINO

1/77 Macleay Street, Potts Point
9331 8333
shop.bottegadelvino.com.au
Open Mon–Fri 10am–9pm,
Sat–Sun 10am–8pm

It might have a modest shopfront and it certainly doesn't shout at you as you walk past, but Bottega del Vino is always bustling. Locals pop into this artisan deli for cheeses, wines, desserts, craft beers, breads and a whole lot more. You can also enjoy some of it on-site; they have seating out the front where you can enjoy people-watching on Macleay Street while devouring some of their tasty menu items. Grab a coffee and some chocolate and enjoy!

4.

GAZEBO
2 Elizabeth Bay Road,
Elizabeth Bay
8070 2424
thegazebo.com.au
Open Mon–Fri 4pm–midnight,
Sun–Sun 12pm–midnight

- -

Gazebo has been going strong since the 1960s and continues to evolve with the times. Before its refurb a few years ago, it was a whimsical wonderland, filled with eclectic objects and a taxidermied fox that hung from the roof. Its sleek makeover took things in a more dapper direction, though the notorious fox (thankfully) still remains. Its most recent incarnation has made this bar and eatery a slick and sophisticated affair; ideal for sipping and socialising in. It is made for summer soirees, with an outside bar that overlooks Fitzroy Gardens across the road.

HOT TIP
The Kings Cross Organic Food Market is just across the road. Check it out on a Saturday morning. It runs from 7.30am to 2pm.

5.

JIMMY LIKS
186–188 Victoria Street,
Potts Point
8354 1400
jimmyliks.com.au
Open Mon–Sat 5pm–late,
Sun 12pm–late

You get hit with a feeling when you walk past Jimmy Liks of an evening that tastes suspiciously like jealousy. There's an energy and a vibe pouring out of this intimate bar that you really want to be a part of. A long wooden table dominates the interior and sets the scene for communal dining. But there are spaces around it that are made for more private date nights or afternoon tipples. The fare is Asian-inspired hawker food and is ideal for sharing, but you can pop in to enjoy happy hour without eating and simply soak up the atmosphere.

6.

KINGSLEYS STEAK AND CRABHOUSE
The Wharf, Cowper Wharf
Road, Woolloomooloo
1300 546 475
kingsleys.com.au
Open Mon–Sat 12pm–late,
Sun 12pm–9pm

Woolloomooloo's iconic wharf is filled with upmarket restaurants. But sometimes you just want a killer steak in comfortable surrounds. Kingsleys gives you all that and more. The setting is still sophisticated, of course, but the food is far more relaxed and the decor is wonderfully dapper. Think dark wooden tables, padded booths adorned in aged leather and industrial pendant lights. All of that is inside, though. The best seats in the house are outside on the wharf, where you can watch the lights of the city skyline flicker in front of you.

5.

6.

MS G'S

155 Victoria Street, Potts Point
8313 1000
merivale.com.au/msgs
Open Mon–Thurs 5pm–midnight,
Fri 12pm–midnight,
Sat 5pm–1am, Sun 1–10pm

The food at Ms G's is like nothing you've ever encountered. Ever. The menu items seem completely weird and wacky at first glance, but they're an absolute knockout on the way down. The Thai green curry jaffle is the perfect example of unexpected deliciousness, while the cheeseburger spring rolls are a true revelation. The venue is a cool mix of industrial and urban, with exposed brick, giant wall murals, glass jars stuck to ceilings and neon signs adorning the walls. It's an eclectic decor mix that perfectly mirrors the menu. This will be your new favourite.

PEEKABOOS
120 Bourke Street,
Woolloomooloo
0403 747 788
peekaboobar.net.au
Open Tues–Thurs 4–10pm,
Fri–Sat 4pm–12am

Dimly lit of an evening but
loud in every other way,
Peekaboos is a nice escape
from the more upmarket bars
that dominate Woolloomooloo.
The team here are experts
in cocktails and the food is
an ever-revolving slew of
canapés. You never really
know what's coming next in
this bar, which is a welcome
change in a suburb that's
becoming a tad predictable.
The back wall, which is
covered in quotes and
illustrations of old Hollywood
greats, is also pretty cool.

Imogene Roache is a freelance interior and food stylist who has spent years scouring Sydney for phenomenal photo shoot locations. She also sources props for her shoots in the area and has become an expert on where the locals go to eat, drink and spend some cash.

Best weekend brunch spot?

Room 10 on Llankelly Place in Potts Point is always a favourite of mine. Further up the road is The Goodwill Society; great coffee, prime location and a cute rustic fit-out.

Where do you love to shop?

Becker Minty (*see* page 148) is an absolute dream to shop in, and also one of my favourite places to source in for photo shoots. Every object they sell is luxurious and special, and sourced from all around the world.

The best place to be at cocktail hour?

I'm loving Riley Street Garage at the moment, in Woolloomooloo. Everything from their pretty cocktail list, to the beautifully converted art deco building.

Escaping the rat race

My aunty lives in Musswellbrook in the upper Hunter Valley, which is where I like to get away when I have any spare time. She owns a thoroughbred horse breeding and racing operation up there. Seeing the beautiful horses and staying in such an open country space is completely different to the city, which is what I love most.

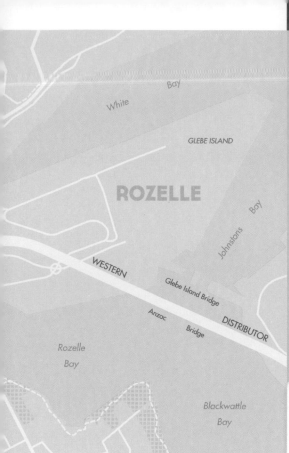

Head down Market Street in the CBD and you'll eventually hit the Pyrmont Bridge. It's the gateway to the other side of the harbour, where a host of dining venues await you. On the Pyrmont side of the water you can take in the city skyline from your restaurant table – nothing beats it. Pyrmont features an interesting mix of people: part work brigade, a few cool kids, tourists and some seasoned locals.

Walk a little further around the Pyrmont side of the harbour and you'll hit Haymarket. The cuisine here is predominantly Asian, and authentically amazing. It's far cheaper to dine in Haymarket too, but don't be fooled by the ordinary decor in some eateries. The food will make up for it.

SHOP
1 The Spa at The Darling
2 Sydney Fish Market

EAT
3 Adriano Zumbo
4 Mamak
EAT AND DRINK
5 Flying Fish
6 Lumi
7 Sokyo

PYRMONT AND HAYMARKET

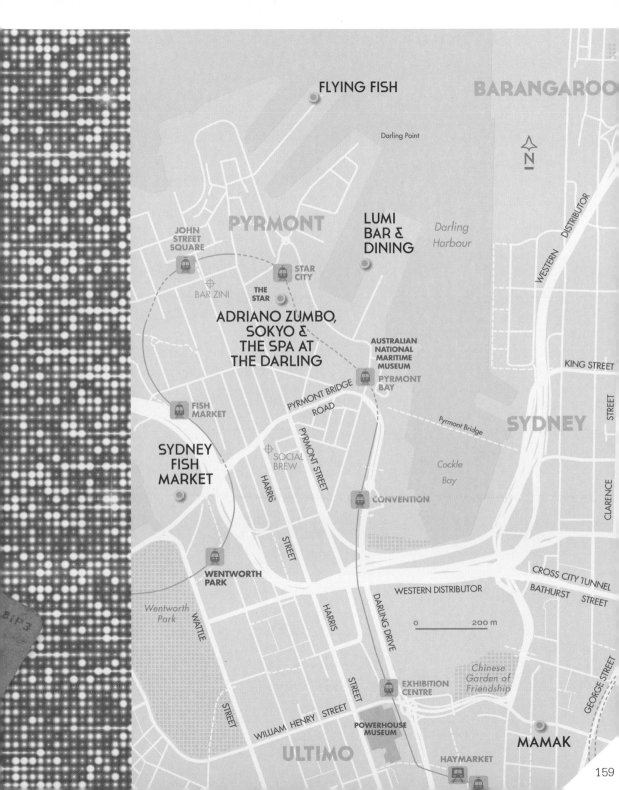

FLYING FISH

BARANGAROO

Darling Point

N

PYRMONT

LUMI BAR & DINING

Darling Harbour

JOHN STREET SQUARE

BAR ZINI

STAR CITY

THE STAR

ADRIANO ZUMBO, SOKYO & THE SPA AT THE DARLING

AUSTRALIAN NATIONAL MARITIME MUSEUM

PYRMONT BAY

KING STREET

WESTERN DISTRIBUTOR

SYDNEY

STREET

FISH MARKET

PYRMONT BRIDGE ROAD

Pyrmont Bridge

SOCIAL BREW

PYRMONT STREET

Cockle Bay

CLARENCE

SYDNEY FISH MARKET

HARRIS

CONVENTION

STREET

WENTWORTH PARK

Wentworth Park

HARRIS

DARLING DRIVE

WESTERN DISTRIBUTOR

CROSS CITY TUNNEL

BATHURST STREET

0   200 m

WATTLE

STREET

Chinese Garden of Friendship

GEORGE STREET

STREET

WILLIAM HENRY STREET

EXHIBITION CENTRE

POWERHOUSE MUSEUM

MAMAK

ULTIMO

HAYMARKET

1.

THE SPA AT THE DARLING

Level 2, The Star,
80 Pyrmont Street, Pyrmont
9657 8088
thedarling.com.au
Open Mon–Thurs 9am–8pm,
Fri–Sun 9am–9pm

- -

The Star is a big-partying casino, but when it's time to unwind from the night before, the who's who are at the casino's on-site retreat, The Spa. Located within The Darling Hotel on level 2, this 14-room sanctuary offers luxury facials, massage and body treatments, as well as a host of other 5-star indulgences. You don't need to be staying at The Star to enjoy it either, so I'd highly recommend an afternoon of pampering (just ensure you book ahead).

SYDNEY FISH MARKET

Bank Street and Pyrmont
Bridge Road, Pyrmont
9004 1108
sydneyfishmarket.com.au
Open Mon–Thurs 7am–4pm,
Fri–Sun 7am–5pm

The Sydney Fish Market is iconic, and it's often heaving with crowds looking to get the best in local seafood. But it's not all markets. This destination houses small food courts and cafes, sushi bars, gift shops, wine stores and some amazing restaurants. Try **Doyle's at Sydney Fish Markets** for exquisite seafood, or for yum cha you can't go past **Fisherman's Wharf Seafood Restaurant**. If you want to keep it cheap and cheerful, grab some fish and chips and sit by the water; you can watch boats come in and the views are amazing.

HOT TIP
If you are after seafood to take away, go early. It's first in best dressed.

3.
ADRIANO ZUMBO

Shop 1, Cafe Court, The Star,
80 Pyrmont Street, Pyrmont
1900 858 611
adrianozumbo.com
Open Mon 11am–10pm,
Tues–Thurs 11am–11pm,
Fri–Sat 11am–midnight,
Sun 11am–9pm

Watching chefs in restaurants
prepare your food is fun
and all, but it's definitely
taken to the next level when
it's cakes, macarons and
other confectionery they're
creating. That's what's in
store when you pop into
Adriano Zumbo. This is
a mecca for lovers of all
things sweet, where you
can get a selection of your
fave macarons, chocolates
and more packaged up
(as a gift or for yourself –
no judgement).

4.
MAMAK

12 Goulburn Street, Haymarket
9211 1668
mamak.com.au
Open Mon–Sun 11.30am–
2.30pm, 5.30pm–10pm

People queue for 30 minutes
or more outside this venue
to get in some nights, so it's
wise to allow time, but at
least there's a chef preparing
fresh roti you can watch
through the front window.
Once you're in, you'll realise
what everyone's going on
about and why there are
three of these restaurants.
The decor is humble and
fuss-free, allowing the
vast and varied menu of
spectacular roti, spicy
delights, rice and noodle
dishes and more to be the
stars of the show. It's an
impressive art.

5.

FLYING FISH

Jones Bay Wharf,
19–21 Pirrama Road, Pyrmont
9518 6677
flyingfish.com.au
Open Tues–Sun 12–2.30pm,
Mon–Sat 6–10.30pm

It's not until you're sitting at Flying Fish, casting your eyes over the Harbour Bridge, that you realise how special the waterfront view here is. But it's not just about the view – the menu is innovative and ever changing, with curries and Asian-inspired dishes mixed in with seafood and other contemporary delights. The rustic decor and carefully considered mood lighting also make the place pretty stellar. And that view just makes everything magical.

LUMI

56 Pirrama Road, Pyrmont
9571 1999
lumidining.com
Open Thurs–Sun 12pm–
2.30pm, Wed–Sun 6–10pm

Lumi is a fine-dining venue, but a relaxed one without pretension – it has an indoor-meets-out vibe that you can't help but get excited about. It's intimate, yet wonderfully alfresco! The location alone – perched right on the wharf and just across from The Star – makes eating here an experience you shouldn't miss. The decor is mid-century modern, with a bouquet of plant and flower varieties adorning the dining room. The à la carte menu is just as delicious as the fit-out, with options like beef cheek, lamb cutlet Milanese style and burnt semolina spaghetti.

7.

SOKYO

Level G, The Darling at The Star,
80 Pyrmont Road, Pyrmont
1800 700 700
star.com.au
Daily 7–10.30am, Fri–Sat
12–2.30pm, Sun–Wed
5.30–9.30pm, Thurs–Sat
5.30–10.30pm

It's really hard not to be taken
aback by the decor in Sokyo –
in a good way. Before you
even think about the menu
you'll need to get past the
giant installation of rope that
hangs from the roof in one
section. It's pretty mind-
blowing. While the design is
dark and moody, the food is
anything but. The sashimi
is to die for, the tempura is
heavenly and the dessert
menu is brimming with sweet
treats. Go for the dessert
alone. And the design. Did
I mention the design?

HOT TIP
Not hungry? Sit in the bar area and enjoy a saké. They also do lunch specials.

Thomas Towhidi is one half of popular home decor brand Urban Couture. He's taken the local design world by storm alongside partner Katriarna Rodgers. With a warehouse in Pyrmont (and a new store in Surry Hills you should definitely check out), it was only fitting I ask Thomas to name some of his fave venues in the area.

Best place to go for dinner in the area?

We would definitely have to say Sokyo (*see* page 166). Having been a regular at Toko in Surry Hills for a few years, we were over the moon when Sokyo popped up around the corner. The sushi is amazing and the chefs are incredibly talented. Bar Zini is also a great option for a mid-week Italian dinner. The boys there can really serve up a great pasta and wine.

Where do you go for a caffeine hit?

Our local coffee haunt is Social Brew. The baristas there are great and it has a really energetic feel to it.

When it's time to shop

Due to Pyrmont's geographical location, you're only a nice 10–15 minute walk away from shopping in the CBD, in particular Pitt Street Mall.

Getting out of the city

To get away from the hustle and bustle of the city, Kat and I both love to head up to Palm Beach for the weekend. It's only about an hour's drive and is the perfect place for a swim and some brunch at The Boathouse (*see* page 116).

About 10 years ago, Redfern and Waterloo were a little rough around the edges. But now, thanks to the volume of apartment buildings and multi-arts centre Carriageworks, this precinct is revitalised and is a drinking and dining mecca for all the cool cats. Redfern is a traditionally Aboriginal suburb, and the mix of cultures has brought out the best in the area.

It's easy to walk and there's plenty of foot traffic and public transport. Seasoned locals mingle with the young and hip, making it a diverse area to play in. All of the venues are free of pretense. Of course, locals who have lived there all their lives will tell you that it was always this good. They might be right.

REDFERN AND WATERLOO

/HOP
1 Doug Up on Bourke
2 /easonal Concepts

EAT
3 The Eathouse Diner
4 /cout's Honour
5 White Rabbit Gallery
DRINK
6 Arcadia Liquors
7 The Dock

WHITE
RABBIT
GALLERY

CHIPPENDALE

CLEVELAND
STREET

ABERCROMBIE
STREET

Prince
Alfred
Park

CLEVELAND

CHALMERS
STREET

ELIZABETH
STREET

STREET

SURRY
HILLS

Ward
Park

STREET

REDFERN

THE
DOCK

ARCADIA
LIQUORS

SEASONAL
CONCEPTS

RETRO ON
REGENT

SCOUT'S
HONOUR

TAPEO

EATHOUSE
DINER

STREET

REDFERN

THE BEARDED TIT

Redfern
Park

FINISHING
TOUCHES
RESTORATIONS

Redfern
Oval

0   200 m

RAGLAN

BOTANY

STREET

ELIZABETH

WATERLOO

WYNDHAM

ROAD

Mount
Carmel
Reserve

STREET

MCEVOY

DOUG
UP ON
BOURKE

BOURKE
STREET

MCEVOY
STREET

LACHLAN
STREET

BOTANY

STREET

Waterloo
Park

STREET

ELIZABETH

BOURKE

O'DEA

AVENUE

N

ROAD

STREET

ZETLAND

171

1.

DOUG UP ON BOURKE

901 Bourke Street, Waterloo
0000 0000
douguponbourke.com.au
Open Tues–Sat 10am–5pm

Imagine the most massive vintage emporium you can. Now, multiply that by 10. That's how overwhelmingly grand Doug Up on Bourke is. Filled to the brim with items that have been dug up from all over the country, this is a hardcore collectables warehouse on a mammoth scale. Going strong since 2003, it's the place to go for antiques, oddities, rare furniture, rustic homeware finds and more. The giant taxidermy camel that sits inside is just the encore. Doug not only sells just about anything you could think of, but also hires out its unique props to stylists and movie makers.

2.

SEASONAL CONCEPTS

122 Redfern Street, Redfern
0400 044 000
seasonalconcepts.com.au
Open Tues–Sat 10am–5pm,
Mon by appointment

Visiting Seasonal Concepts is almost like going through the cupboard into Narnia. It's a majestic and moody destination filled with old wares and wonders, where many local stylists can be found hiring props for photo shoots and movies. There's a little bit of everything inside, but the most startling is the giant taxidermy heads on the wall towards the back of the store. You'll also spot fresh flowers on sale, curiosities for the kitchen and a few toys and other assorted bric-a-brac that are sure to give you childhood flashbacks (and handily fit in your suitcase).

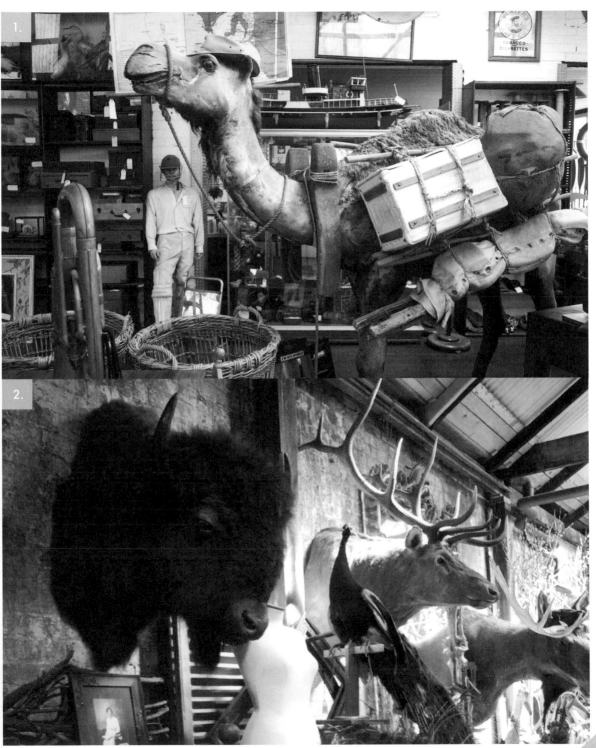

1.

2.

3.

THE EATHOUSE DINER
302 Chalmers Street, Redfern
8084 0470
eathousediner.com.au
Open Mon–Sat from 5pm,
Sat and Sun 9am–3pm

The mint and red exterior of this retro diner suggests that you're in for a colourful experience. This colour extends inside all the way to the toilets, which are clad in naughty posters. Cheeky! Open for brunch, lunch and dinner, Eathouse Diner is best visited at night, when the humble menu plays second fiddle to the extensive drinks list. It has an electric atmosphere almost as vibrant as its colourful walls – and with tasty plates you can share or savour alone. Winning dishes from the menu are the chipotle chicken, spiced lamb mince shakshouka and the banana split dessert.

HOT TIP
Head in between 5pm and 7pm and enjoy their happy hour cocktail prices.

SCOUT'S HONOUR
118 George Street, Redfern
0421 203 382
Open Mon–Fri 7am–3pm,
Sat 8am–2.30pm

Any cafe that has an adorable dog waiting outside to greet you is a winner in my books, and that's the welcome you'll get at this cafe. It's tight on space inside this former fruit shop – there's no denying it – but they do a lot with what they've got. Locals tend to order take-away coffees and bites, but it is worth securing a spot in the dining space at the back just to watch the staff whip up their sandwiches, salads and cakes. The cakes are particularly divine.

5.

WHITE RABBIT GALLERY

30 Balfour Street, Chippendale
8399 2867
whiterabbitcollection.org
Open Wed–Sun 10am–5pm

While it's not technically in this precinct, White Rabbit Gallery is too good not to showcase. Open since 2009 in the neighbouring suburb of Chippendale, it's become the go-to hub for lovers of contemporary Chinese art, with two major exhibitions happening every year. It also features an on-site tea house, with a wide variety of Chinese and Taiwanese tea. They have beautiful flower teas that blossom in the pot and some thirst-quenching cooling lychee tea. You can enjoy a plate of handmade dumplings, which are pretty extraordinary teamed with the wine or beer.

6.

ARCADIA LIQUORS

7 Cope Street, Redfern
8068 4170
arcadialiquors.com
Open Mon–Fri 4pm–midnight,
Sat 12pm–midnight,
Sun 12–10pm

A beer garden where your dog is allowed to sit with you while you drink is just one of the things that makes this Redfern watering hole such a popular hangout. Some might consider it a hipster bar due to its salvage-shop aesthetic and menu of toasted sandwiches, but there's definitely more at play here. This is a laid-back pub that doesn't take itself too seriously. Pop in any night of the week and expect to see a busy bar, bustling beer garden and the occasional live band playing inside the door. You'll feel like a local even if it's your first visit.

THE DOCK
182 Redfern Street, Redfern
8034 3654
thedockredfern.com
Open Mon–Sat 12pm–12am,
Sun 12–10pm

Going to a friend's house party is the best way to describe visiting The Dock; it's crammed full of people on busier nights and is so relaxed you could almost pour your own beer (but resist the urge). Run by two local lads, this somewhat ramshackle bar is all about the drinking, but does do the occasional bite. You can even bring your own food. It's a little anything goes, with the occasional sing-along taking place that everyone can get involved in. The Dock features chalk-covered walls, vintage pendant lamps and exposed brick, and is definitely a nook you can spend a few hours curled up in.

Sharon Farrell is the creative genius behind Sharon the Makeup Artist; a blog and YouTube channel that has taken the country by storm. She's lived in Redfern for a few years now, and as an Irish lass she's more than sorted out the best places to drink, dine and shop.

Where will we find you enjoying a drink?

I love the Bearded Tit on Regent Street. It's equally good for a quiet after-work tipple, or a crazy Saturday night out with friends. The drinks selection is great but not overwhelming, and the eclectic decor will give you lots to talk about with your mates!

Best place to grab a bite in the area?

Tapeo on Redfern Street is always a safe bet for a slap-up meal with a Spanish Twist. The menu changes often to reflect what's in season, and always has an interesting mix of tapas and more traditional restaurant favourites.

Any must-see stores?

It's quite amazing how many furniture and homewares shops are crammed into a small area. Take a stroll down Regent Street and pop into Finishing Touches Restorations to marvel at the work of the restoration team. A little further down the street is Retro on Regent; a great spot to pick up a pair of vintage flamingos for your front lawn.

Where do you relax outside of the city?

My favourite getaway is three hours south down the coast at Jervis Bay. The beaches are honestly the most beautiful I have ever seen and there's plenty of bars and restaurants to visit in the evenings.

Rose Bay, Watsons Bay and the suburbs between them are some of Sydney's most affluent and picturesque. The cafes and restaurants, with their historic and visually stunning settings overlooking the harbour, are really special.

Seeing the best sights is as easy as jumping on the ferry or driving east from the city for 30 minutes. New South Head Road extends from Rose Bay all the way to Watsons Bay and you need only take a few turns off it to explore some amazing places.

The landscape here makes you feel like you've almost escaped into another world, with some buildings dating back to the 19th century. Continue the old-world feel by taking a picnic (or fish and chips!) to yacht-watch in Rose Bay's Lyne Park.

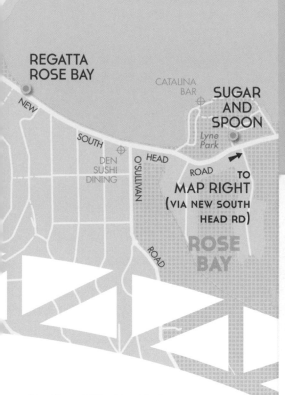

EAT
1 Doyles on the Beach
2 Sugar and Spoon
3 Vaucluse House Tearooms

EAT AND DRINK
4 Dunbar House
5 Regatta Rose Bay
6 Watsons Bay Boutique Hotel

ROSE BAY TO WATSONS BAY

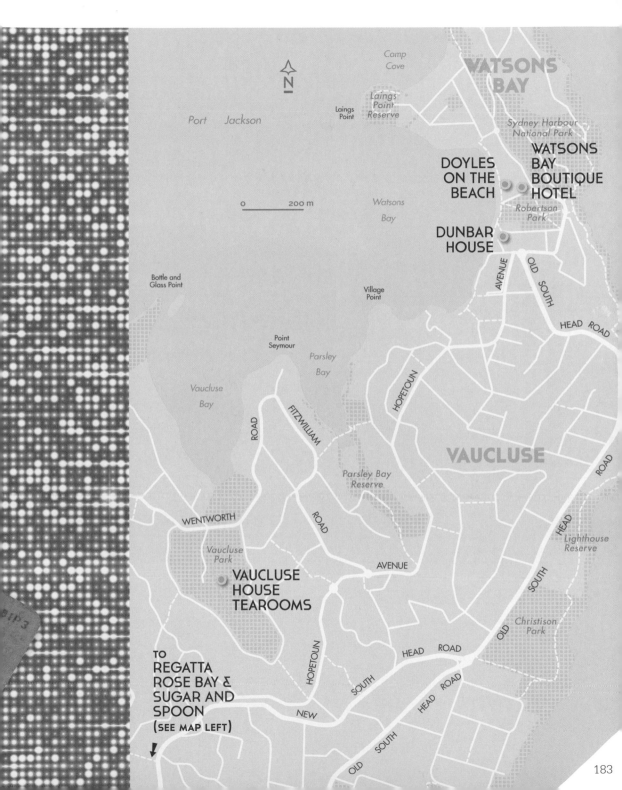

N

Port Jackson

Camp
Cove

Laings
Point

Laings
Point
Reserve

**WATSONS
BAY**

Sydney Harbour
National Park

0   200 m

Watsons
Bay

**DOYLES
ON THE
BEACH**

**WATSONS
BAY
BOUTIQUE
HOTEL**

Robertson
Park

**DUNBAR
HOUSE**

AVENUE

OLD SOUTH

HEAD ROAD

Bottle and
Glass Point

Village
Point

HOPETOUN

Point
Seymour

Parsley
Bay

VAUCLUSE

Vaucluse
Bay

ROAD

FITZWILLIAM

Parsley Bay
Reserve

ROAD

HEAD

WENTWORTH

ROAD

Vaucluse
Park

AVENUE

Lighthouse
Reserve

**VAUCLUSE
HOUSE
TEAROOMS**

SOUTH

OLD

Christison
Park

HOPETOUN

SOUTH

HEAD ROAD

**TO
REGATTA
ROSE BAY &
SUGAR AND
SPOON**
(SEE MAP LEFT)

NEW

HEAD ROAD

OLD SOUTH

1.

DOYLES ON THE BEACH

11 Marine Parade, Watsons Bay
9337 2007
doyles.com.au
Open Mon–Fri 12–3pm,
Sat–Sun 12–4pm, Fri–Sat
5.30–9pm, Sun to Thurs
5.30–8.30pm

It's no easy feat in Sydney to find a venue with as much history as Doyles on the Beach. This restaurant is an undisputed icon of Sydney and is well over 100 years old. That aside, it's the casual vibe and seafood that keeps the locals coming back. It's literally situated on the beach, so you can sit at a table and watch the waves roll in. It's the kind of spot you'll want to have a wine at of an afternoon – seafood lunch essential – and never leave.

SUGAR AND SPOON
600 New South Head Road,
Rose Bay
9388 3834
Open Mon–Sun 7am–5pm

Water views in Rose Bay don't come more relaxed and family-friendly than the ones at Sugar and Spoon. With a nearby playground and a kids' menu, it's little wonder it's the go-to spot for mums and bubs. The fit-out is just as understated and chilled out as the atmosphere, so you can enjoy the all-day breakfast for hours – especially if you secure one of the sought-after outdoor tables.

HOT TIP
Sugar and Spoon sits right on the edge of Lyne Park; perfect for a post-feed stroll.

3.
VAUCLUSE HOUSE TEAROOMS

Wentworth Road, Vaucluse
9388 8188
vauclusehousetearooms.com.au
Open Wed–Fri 10am–4.30pm,
Sat–Sun 8am–4.30pm

Before you even go inside the grand and historic sandstone building that houses Vaucluse House Tearooms, you'll feel like you're in a scene from a movie. With 10 hectares of picturesque gardens that reach all the way to Sydney Harbour, just driving towards the building is a breathtaking experience. Inside the cafe, it's not all cucumber sandwiches, with hearty meals on offer and a menu for the kids. You should go of a morning as it's the perfect spot for paper reading and garden roaming.

4.
DUNBAR HOUSE

9 Marine Parade, Watsons Bay
9337 1226
dunbarhouse.com.au
Open Mon–Sun from 8am

Whoever came up with the idea to open a cafe inside well-established wedding venue Dunbar House a few years ago needs to be thanked. The interior is stunning, the food is sublime and the views are second-to-none. The old-meets-new design scheme inside this venue gives design nerds (like yours truly) the best of both worlds. Be sure to grab something from Dunbar's breakfast or lunch menu (the Devonshire tea and finger sandwiches are very appropriate), or treat yourself to their indulgent desserts instead – coconut and white chocolate pannacotta, please!

HOT TIP

There's always an event going on at Dunbar House, so you might catch a wedding reception arrival while you sip on your Chardonnay.

3.

4.

4.

5.

REGATTA ROSE BAY

594 New South Head Road,
Rose Bay
9327 6561
regattarosebay.com
Open Thurs–Sun 12–3pm,
Wed–Sat 6pm–late

Situated on the Rose Bay
Pier, Regatta is all water
views, featuring a stellar
dining room that's saturated
with light during the day.
It's definitely the place to
be (wine in hand) as you
overlook the marina of
yachts. Of a night, hop in
for dinner and enjoy the
backdrop of glittering stars.
It's pretty hard to fault this
venue, and the menu of surf
and turf delights is the icing
on the cake. Dishes like
pan-roasted barramundi or
braised short rib feature on
their evolving menu – and
the pistachio brûlée tart is
heaven-sent, too.

6.

WATSONS BAY BOUTIQUE HOTEL

1 Military Road, Watsons Bay
9337 5444
watsonsbayhotel.com.au
Open Mon–Sat 10am–12am,
Sun 10am–10pm

Some venues are sickeningly
stunning – and this one is
that and more. The decor is
so phenomenal you could
feast on it alone. The Beach
Club is the best spot in the
house, decked out with mint
green paint, coconuts and
pineapples. There's also the
more subdued Sunset Room
and dreamy accommodation.
Hands-down one of Sydney's
greatest venues, you can dine
here for breakfast, lunch and
dinner. The food is traditional
(think beer-battered fish and
chips or lamb shank), and
the tasty kids' menu means
it's a relaxing affair for the
whole family.

5.

6.

HOT TIP
Get the ferry from Circular Quay if you're keen for an afternoon of bites and bevvies

MEET THE SYDNEYSIDER
SARAH CICHY
PR MAVEN

Sarah Cichy spends her days looking after a slew of creative PR clients and it only made sense to get her take on some of the best venues in her area. A former Melburnian, Sarah now calls Rose Bay home and has enjoyed getting acquainted with its stores, cafes and restaurants the past few years.

What's your number one dinner destination in the area?

You'll most likely see me three or more times a week at Den Sushi Dining, Rose Bay, for either lunch or dinner. It's incredibly relaxed and probably some of the best sushi I've ever had.

Where does one go for an evening tipple?

Catalina Bar has a beautiful outdoor area overlooking the bay. My favourite cocktail is their espresso martini. But be warned – there's no decaf option, so prepare to stay awake for a little longer!

What does a day out in the suburb look like?

Most Sundays we'll round up a group of friends for a long lunch/ early dinner at Watsons Bay Boutique Hotel (*see* page 189), which has casual alfresco dining and is a short drive from the city (so it feels like we've escaped for the afternoon).

Best place to shop?

Parisi's Foodhall has the freshest fruit and veggies. I'm there every second day topping up our fruit bowl.

Where do you escape to outside of Sydney?

Church Point Boathouse, Pittwater. It's an old-school milk bar with a divine little bottle shop and seafood restaurant attached to it.

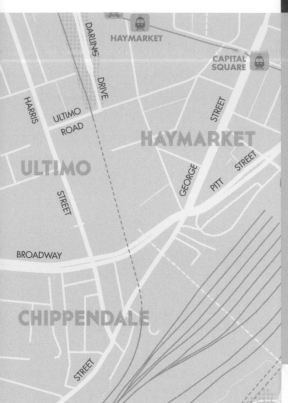

Sydneysiders know that Surry Hills is the place to be. It has a tonne of slick venues without pretension, and its proximity to Oxford Street's club scene makes it a fun hub to play in with friends. This precinct is made for bar hopping, and with all-day breakfast on offer in so many excellent cafes you can nurse that hangover in style.

The main streets – Cleveland and Crown – hold many of the precinct's best places to dine, and there's also a slew of amazing stores. Wander off the beaten track because side streets in Surry Hills are laden with boutiques and cafes.

24   JUN 8076

SHOP
1 Surry Hills Shopping
EAT
2 Bills
3 Gelato Messina
4 The Nepalese Kitchen

17

EAT AND DRINK
5 The Beresford
6 Bodega
7 The Winery

SURRY HILLS

WENTWORTH AV

SPICE I AM

Harmony Park

CAMPBELL

STREET

OXFORD

STREET

DISTRIBUTOR

ELIZABETH STREET

ALBION

STREET

0   100 m

SURRY
HILLS

STREET

EASTERN

OXFORD

STREET

THE
WINERY

HOLY
KITSCH

CROWN

FLINDERS

COMMONWEALTH STREET

BODEGA

ALBION

THE
BERESFORD

STREET

STREET

FOVEAUX

STREET

BILLS

STREET

SOUTH DOWLING

STREET

STREET

FOVEAUX

GELATO
MESSINA

STREET

SOMEDAYS

FITZROY

SURRY HILLS
MARKETS

CITTA
DESIGN

STREET

BOURKE

CLOCK
HOTEL

COLLECTOR
STORE

SUZUYA

N

Ward Park

KIDO

TITLE

PAPER 2

DISTRIBUTOR

STREET

DOWLING

ANZAC

Moore
Park

PARADE

THE
STANDARD
STORE

THE
NEPALESE
KITCHEN

STREET

EASTERN

SOUTH

Moore
Park

CLEVELAND

STREET

CROWN

CLEVELAND

STREET

MOORE
PARK

REDFERN

ERCIYES

SURRY HILLS SHOPPING

Get off the bus at the start of Crown Street and make a day of exploring the shops. On this busy main strip, pop your head into **Paper 2** for a good dose of stationery. This local favourite is owned by graphic designer Margaret Rockliff and it's filled with paper creations from all over the world.

Kido Store is just steps away and is the best place to get kids' clothing, bedding, bath and body products. Many of their items are organic and the family who runs the store travel extensively to bring the world's best brands back to Sydney.

Just up the street you'll find **Holy Kitsch**, which is like walking into a cupboard full of kooky and crazy trinkets. It stocks jewellery, Mexican art, skulls, toys, mugs and a host of other weird and wonderful gifts.

Fashion lovers will lose their minds in boutiques like **Somedays** (Fitzroy Street) and **The Standard Store**. The former stocks casual men's and women's clothing in a fairly black, grey and white colour palette (with some killer watches thrown in for good measure), while the latter is a hip and cool urban paradise with clothing for guys and girls. They have some ripper sunglasses you should definitely check out.

Collector Store is a boutique that supports local and emerging brands. It's filled with men's and women's clothing, homewares, and other goodies like photography, art and jewellery.

For an unbeatable community feel and to pick up some amazing vintage clothing (as well as decor, books, gifts and more), you have to check out the **Surry Hills Markets**. They run on the first Saturday of each month in Shannon Reserve (on Crown Street beside The Clock Hotel).

Design lovers should drift over to Bourke Street and check out **Citta Design**. It's a mecca for furniture and homewares with an international feel, but also stocks clothing, soft furnishings and other items you can squeeze in a suitcase.

FUN WITH WASHI

BILLS

359 Crown Street
9360 4762
bills.com.au
Open Mon–Fri 7am–10pm,
Sat–Sun 7.30am–10pm

It's always a good sign when a cafe is busy from the moment its doors swing open and Bills on Crown falls into that category. The creation of chef and food writer Bill Granger, this venue serves up classics around the clock, with a wonderfully simple breakfast, lunch and dinner menu. The ricotta hotcakes are hard to pass up of a morning, while the lunch menu boasts sumptuous creations like the yellow fish curry. For dinner, you could make a meal out of the small plates alone – bring on the calamari, tempura prawns and zucchini fritters.

3.

GELATO MESSINA
389 Crown Street
gelatomessina.com
Open Sun–Thurs 12–11pm,
Fri and Sat 12–11.30pm

If you're wandering along Crown Street and spot a line of people, they're not trying to get into a nightclub; they're queuing to get a taste of Gelato Messina. It seems like this place never calms down, even though the gelato craze hit a few years back and appears to have died off elsewhere. With divine desserts made from scratch, special flavours released each week and a total ban on artificial ingredients, the lure of Gelato Messina is powerfully obvious. With up to 40 flavours available on any given visit, this is better than a nightclub – and with no hangover to worry about. The salted caramel and white chocolate gelato is a must-try (and they always allow you to sample a flavour before you commit to it).

4.
THE NEPALESE KITCHEN
481 Crown Street
9319 4264
Open Mon–Sun 5.30–11pm

With so many venues popping up in Surry Hills and leaving shortly after, The Nepalese Kitchen is still going strong after 20 years on Crown Street. Run by a husband and wife team and split over two storeys, it's a humble operation that focuses on great food rather than lavish decor. The menu is brimming with traditional Nepalese fare – and if you haven't tried it before, don't be wary. This restaurant is a place of fragrant curries (try the tomato-based goat curry), a bit of spice and a series of milder dishes (get the handmade vegetable dumplings). The dining room on the ground floor is always pumping – which, in a suburb as competitive as this, is a good sign!

5.
THE BERESFORD
345 Bourke Street
9254 8000
merivale.com.au/
theberesfordhotel
Open Mon–Sun 12pm–1am

Ask any local where you should go for a Sunday afternoon bevvie and they'll tell you to visit The Beresford. Just minutes from the hectic Oxford Street clubs, the giant beer garden out the back of this bar is another world altogether. In the evening it's enchanting as lanterns flick on and the crowd intensifies. This is the place to go for a pre-game drink, birthday celebration or weeknight bite. Disco divas will love the upstairs bar, which is a weekend dance destination. With a menu that's filled with pizza, pasta and more upmarket mains, this has got to be Surry Hills' most versatile, something-for-everyone bar.

4.

5.

6.

BODEGA

216 Commonwealth Street
9212 7766
www.bodegatapas.com
Open Tues–Sat 6pm–late,
Friday 12–3pm, 6pm–late

Take a wander up the hill from Central Station and turn left down Commonwealth Street. It's on this unsuspecting street that you'll discover one of the best dining venues the city fringe has to offer. Complemented by a South American and Spanish wine list, Bodega's food is just as fun and lively as the venue itself, serving up modern tapas dishes like pork sausage in lettuce cups along with share plates like fried-maple beef brisket and mushroom and fontina dumplings. There's also a pretty impressive mural that spans one of the walls inside, and it's just as colourful as the staff. You can't do Surry Hills without experiencing this gem.

HOT TIP
You'll need a reservation;
it's always packed.

THE WINERY
285A Crown Street
8070 2424
thewinerysurryhills.com.au
Open Mon–Fri 6pm–midnight,
Weekends 12pm–midnight

Decked out in gorgeous art deco decor, The Winery is a true vino destination with a huge selection of by-the-glass varieties. Inside, lush greenery dominates the space – along with a little taxidermy – giving the venue an indoor-meets-out ambience with a sophisticated edge, but it's certainly not snooty or pretentious. Upstairs, the Champagne Room is an indulgent delight, with plush velvet booths that feature a 'press for champagne' button. Does it get any better than a flute refill without having to walk to the bar? And, if you're not into drinking, the menu of modern Australian fare is a drawcard too (grilled zucchini lasagne – yes, please!)

PRESS FOR CHAMPAGNE

CHAMPAGNE
PERRIER-JOUËT

Neale Whitaker needs no introduction, but I'll give you a snapshot anyway. Judge on popular TV show *The Block*, former Editor-in-Chief at *Belle* magazine and now taking the reins at *Vogue Living*, he exudes style and sophistication. Who better to comment on the best places to visit in Surry Hills than this design guru?

What are some of your fave dinner destinations in the area?

It depends on mood and budget. Surry Hills is great for good, cheap options. My favourites are Suzuya for Japanese (Devonshire Street), Erciyes for Turkish (Cleveland Street) and Spice I Am for central Thai food (Wentworth Avenue).

Any must-see stores in Surry Hills?

I'm not much of a shopper these days, but I can while away an hour easily in TITLE on Crown Street. First I browse the book side and then the CD and vinyl side. I still love browsing the monthly market on Crown Street. It's been going forever and I've found some treasures over the years.

Best places for a cocktail?

I feel I'm supposed to name some of the cool new laneway bars, but for me it would still have to be the upstairs balcony at the Clock Hotel on Crown Street. Such a great spot on a warm summer night. And the courtyard at The Beresford (*see* page 200). We take our dogs there so it wins hands down.

Where do you go to escape Sydney?

South. To a very secret spot outside Berry at a place called Bundewallah. It's just a dot on the map.

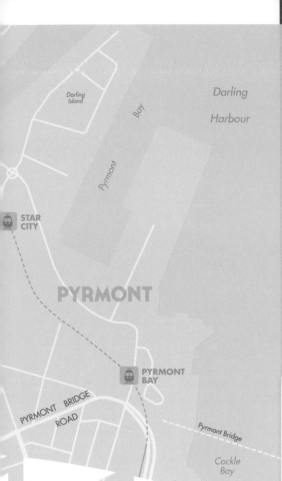

Don't let anyone tell you that the harbour is the only place to be in the Sydney central business district (CBD). Sure, the harbour views are spectacular, but the city, with its mix of historic stone buildings and modern glass towers, won't settle for second place. Add to this local and international designer shops, cafes and restaurants, and you have a world-class city centre.

Take a break from all that shopping and eating with a visit to the Royal Botanic Gardens. Enter via Macquarie Street and get lost among the greenery and glass houses. There are so many paths that all lead in different directions — it's incredibly picturesque.

SHOP
1 CBD Shopping
2 The Strand Arcade
EAT
3 The Tea Room

EAT AND DRINK
4 Cheese & Wine Room
5 Mr Wong's
DRINK
6 The Barbershop
7 Palmer & Co

SYDNEY CBD

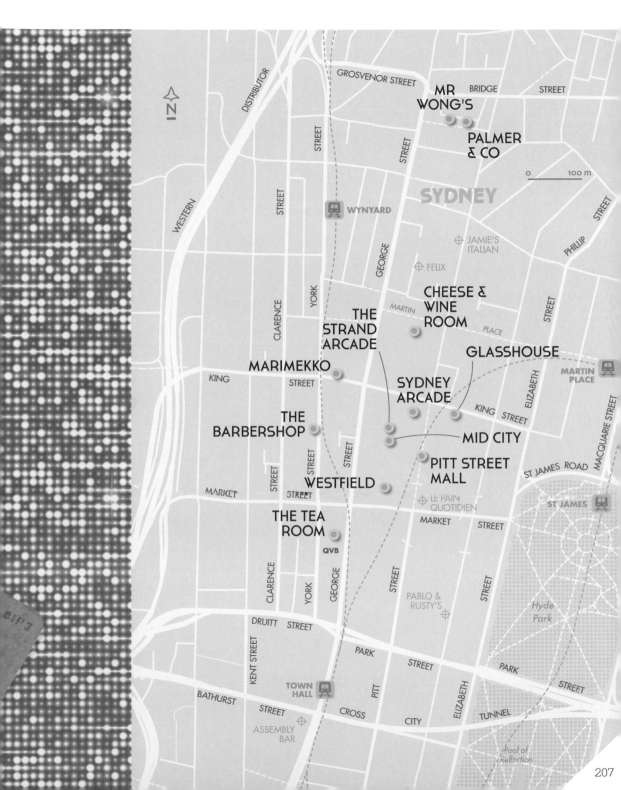

N

GROSVENOR STREET

MR
WONG'S
BRIDGE   STREET

PALMER
& CO

DISTRIBUTOR

WESTERN   STREET

STREET

STREET

WYNYARD

SYDNEY

0   100 m

JAMIE'S
ITALIAN

FELIX

PHILLIP   STREET

GEORGE

CLARENCE

YORK

STREET

MARTIN

CHEESE &
WINE
ROOM

THE
STRAND
ARCADE

PLACE

GLASSHOUSE

MARTIN
PLACE

MARIMEKKO

KING   STREET

SYDNEY
ARCADE

ELIZABETH   STREET

THE
BARBERSHOP

STREET

KING   STREET

MID CITY

WESTFIELD

STREET

PITT STREET
MALL

ST JAMES   ROAD

MACQUARIE STREET

MARKET   STREET

LE PAIN
QUOTIDIEN

ST JAMES

THE TEA
ROOM

QVB

MARKET   STREET

CLARENCE

YORK

GEORGE

STREET

PABLO &
RUSTY'S

Hyde
Park

DRUITT   STREET

KENT STREET

PARK   STREET

PARK   STREET

BATHURST

TOWN
HALL

PITT

ELIZABETH

TUNNEL

STREET   STREET

CROSS

CITY

ASSEMBLY
BAR

Pool of
Reflection

207

1.

CBD SHOPPING

For shopping in the CBD, you can't beat **Pitt Street Mall**; a reasonably small pedestrianised strip that packs a lot in. With hubs like **Glasshouse**, **Sydney Arcade**, **Westfield** and **Mid City** all coming off of it, there's a lot to explore.

Each shopping pocket is slightly different, but the best by far is the recently revamped Westfield shopping centre, which houses designer brands like **Zimmerman**, **Calvin Klein**, **Swarovski**, **Thomas Sabo**, **Armani Exchange** and loads more. You'll also find a gorgeously designed food court on level 5, so you can make a pit-stop to eat and then continue your hunt for the perfect pair of shoes.

The city's two major department stores, **Myer** and **David Jones**, can also be accessed via Westfield, so you really can spend all day shopping.

Wander to nearby King Street if you're a fan of fabrics. **Marimekko** landed in Sydney a few years back and it's two storeys of iconic prints, kitchen and dinnerware, clothing, kids' gear and more.

2.

THE STRAND ARCADE

412–414 George Street, Sydney
9203 0800
strandarcade.com.au
Opening hours Mon–Wed
& Frid 9am–5.30pm,
Thurs 9am–8pm, Sat 9am–4pm,
Sun 11am–4pm

The Strand is an iconic Sydney landmark. Established in 1891, it's the only remaining Victorian arcade left in the city and the architecture is beautiful. This is a charming shopping destination, with the ground floor filled with shops like **Haigh's Chocolates** (for your sweet tooth), **Victoria Buckley** (stunning jewellery) and **Fred Perry** (for on-trend clothing). Go upstairs and the fashion really takes off, with Australian boutiques like **Leona Edmiston**, **Scanlan Theodore**, **The Corner Shop** and **Megan Park** all standouts. If you really want to splurge, head to the top level, where the **Alex Perry** and **Akira** stores live among a slew of other big brands.

1.

1.

2.

1.

2.

2.

3.

THE TEA ROOM
Level 3 North End, Queen
Victoria Building (QVB)
455 George Street, Sydney
9283 7279
thetearoom.com.au
Open Mon–Sun 10am–late

There's no venue in Sydney
quite as grand and quite as
gorgeous as the Tea Room.
Dining in for morning or
afternoon tea here is a bit
of an historical experience,
too. Located in what was
once the original Grand
Ballroom of the QVB (Queen
Victoria Building), the interior
features massive, custom-
designed chandeliers, along
with Victorian ceilings and a
stack of authentic silverware
straight out of Britain. Visit
on the weekend and you
might even see a wedding
reception take place, or
pop-in through the week and
indulge in an à la carte lunch
(with a champagne in hand,
of course!).

4.

CHEESE & WINE ROOM
GPO Grand, 1 Martin Place,
Sydney
9229 7701
gposydney.com/gpo-cheese-
wine-room-sydney
Open Mon–Fri 12–3pm,
Tues–Sat 6–10pm

Cheese lovers will be
experiencing fits of joy and
rapture the moment they
step foot in this romantic
dining space. Situated
underground in the historical
general post office (GPO)
building, this artisan cheese
cellar is the place to go for a
decadent vino and cheese
board. While they do serve
hearty meals from an à la
carte menu, the mammoth
range of cheese and antipasti
(and other gourmet treats) is
hard to pass up. This is the
ultimate date night venue,
but you could go on your
own and have just as much
fun digging into this temple
of cheese.

3.

HOT TIP
There are so many stellar stores in the QVB. Level 2 standouts include Aboriginal Art Galleries (wonderful Indigenous works), Paws a While (memorabilia and gifts for pet owners) and The Art of Dr Seuss store (need we say more?).

4.

5.

MR WONG'S

3 Bridge Lane, Sydney
9240 3000
merivale.com.au/mrwong
Open Mon–Sun 12–3pm,
Mon–Wed 5.30–11pm,
Thurs–Sat 5.30pm–midnight,
Sun 5.30–10pm

Sydney isn't quite as well-known for its secret laneways as Melbourne, but Mr Wong's is changing that. A massive space in a tucked-away laneway, this two-level restaurant does Cantonese-style fare in stunning surrounds (think timber floors, French woven chairs, exposed brick walls and stunning murals – all in a dimly lit setting). The food is just as inspired. Feast on Chinese roasted duck and warm drunken chicken, or opt for seafood sensations like stir-fried black pepper prawns and Balmain bugs with spicy salt. This is premium Chinese dining at its best, but you'd be willing to go just to experience the fit-out.

6.

THE BARBERSHOP
89 York Street, Sydney
9299 9699
thisisthebarbershop.com
Bar open Mon–Tues
4pm–midnight, Wed–Fri
2pm–midnight, Sat 5pm–midnight

It's not everyday you get to have a haircut and then grab a cocktail, but The Barbershop gives you both experiences in a bygone-era setting. Out front, the lads offer a professional grooming service for men, while out back (and with its own separate entrance of an evening), the bar serves up classic Euro drinks for anyone in need of a post-work bevvie. Of a Friday and Saturday night, the bar fills up quickly, and is decked out with old-world decor set against moody green walls.

PALMER & CO
Abercrombie Lane, Sydney
9254 8088
merivale.com.au/palmerandco
Open Sat–Wed 5pm–late,
Thurs–Fri 3pm–late

Your phone reception might drop out once you venture down the stairs of this underground bar, but you tend to forget about the city above once you're inside. This prohibition-style bar has staff decked out as dapper gents and flapper waitresses, and a menu packed with seasonal drinks so good they are almost criminal – but nothing feels themed or kitsch. It's the perfect balance of refinement and debauchery and you can't find anything else like it in Sydney.

MEET THE SYDNEYSIDER
TARA DENNIS
INTERIOR DESIGN QUEEN

When Tara Dennis is not completing a makeover or craft project on TV's *Better Homes & Gardens*, she's out and about exploring venues in the city with killer decor and an amazing vibe.

What's it like in the heart of the CBD?

I often feel like I have to get really dressed up or else go super casual, there's not much in between. I do love our city though, it's so pretty just to be in Sydney at any time of day.

Best undiscovered bar in the city?

Assembly Bar in Regent Place, just off George Street. They've got great cocktails and a nice selection of wines.

Where do you go for coffee?

Le Pain Quotidien – a cute little French-inspired cafe in Westfield Sydney. They serve lovely little hot chocolates in bowls and the coffee's not bad either. I also like Pablo & Rusty's on Castlereagh Street.

Best places to grab dinner?

Felix in Angel Place and Jamie
Oliver's Jamie's Italian on
Pitt Street.

Where do you go to escape the city?

My house on the Hawkesbury River
is my ultimate weekend escape.
A short drive north, picture perfect
and so peaceful.

The harbour is what makes Sydney a stand-out city. Other cities in Australia have waterways, but none of them come close to this natural magic. Add the historic area of The Rocks and the close-up magnificence of the Harbour Bridge and you have a mix of natural wonder and impressive engineering at every turn in this precinct.

You'll see people jogging along the water, tourists shopping and locals soaking up the sun on lunch breaks. You'll spot just as many buskers as you do seagulls. At night, lights flicker, ferries drop locals off to wine and dine, and you hear fun and frivolity everywhere around you. There's an energy to this part of Sydney that's intoxicating.

BARANGAROO

Darling

Harbour

SYDNEY

WESTERN DISTRIBUTOR

KOBE JONES

ERSKINE STREET

➡ TO **MAP RIGHT** (VIA ERSKINE, YORK, LANG & HARRINGTON STS)

THE PROMENADE

KING STREET

THE PROMENADE

24   JUN 8076

/HOP
1 MUSEUM OF CONTEMPORARY ART
2 THE ROCKS MARKETS

17

EAT
3 KOBE JONES
4 ANANAS
EAT AND DRINK
5 OPERA BAR
6 THE GLENMORE HOTEL

/YDNEY HARBOUR, CIRCULAR QUAY AND THE ROCKS

CROSS CITY TUNNEL

HARBOUR STREET

BATHURST STREET

GEORGE STREET

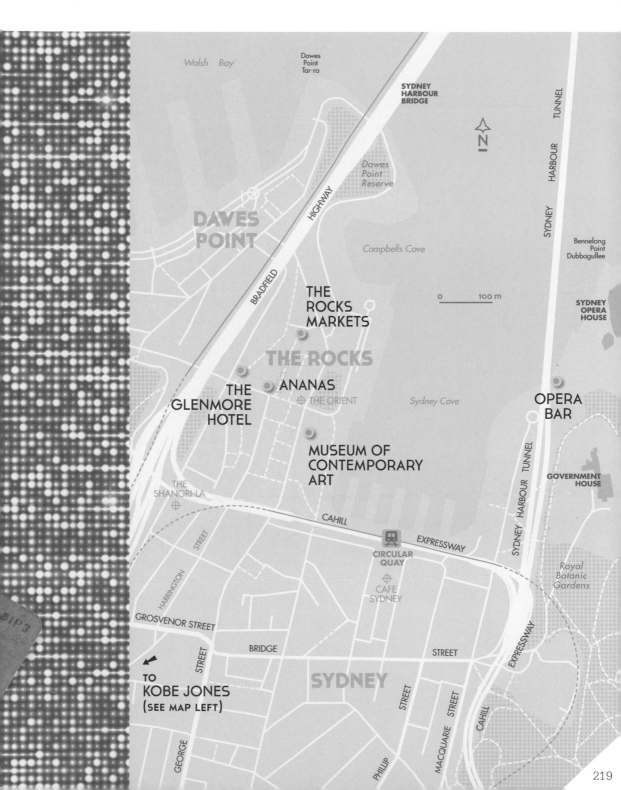

Walsh Bay

Dawes Point Tar-ra

SYDNEY HARBOUR BRIDGE

SYDNEY HARBOUR TUNNEL

Dawes Point Reserve

DAWES POINT

BRADFIELD

HIGHWAY

Campbells Cove

N

Bennelong Point Dubbagullee

SYDNEY OPERA HOUSE

0   100 m

THE ROCKS MARKETS

THE ROCKS

THE GLENMORE HOTEL

ANANAS

THE ORIENT

Sydney Cove

OPERA BAR

MUSEUM OF CONTEMPORARY ART

THE SHANGRI-LA

CAHILL

EXPRESSWAY

SYDNEY HARBOUR TUNNEL

GOVERNMENT HOUSE

CIRCULAR QUAY

CAFE SYDNEY

Royal Botanic Gardens

GROSVENOR STREET

STREET

HARRINGTON

BRIDGE

STREET

STREET

SYDNEY

EXPRESSWAY

TO KOBE JONES
(SEE MAP LEFT)

GEORGE

PHILLIP

STREET

MACQUARIE STREET

CAHILL

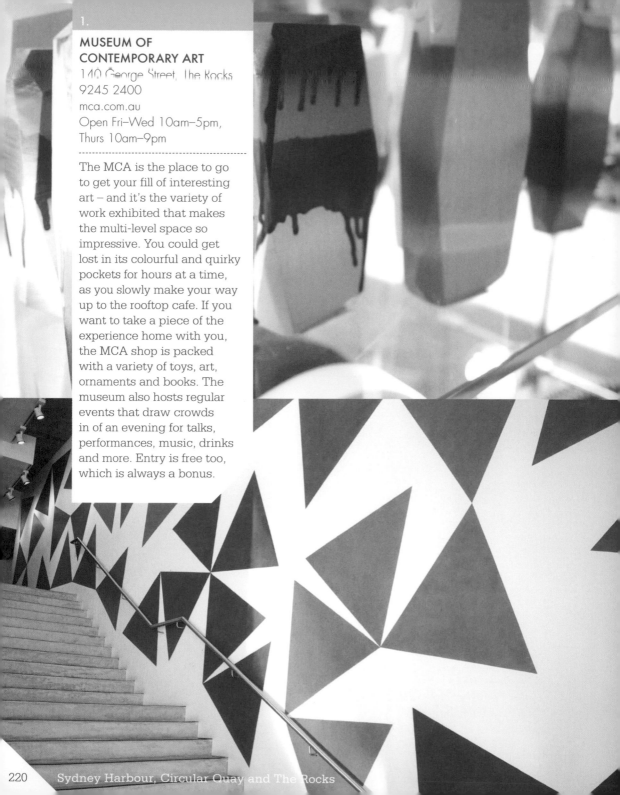

1.

MUSEUM OF CONTEMPORARY ART

140 George Street, The Rocks
9245 2400
mca.com.au
Open Fri–Wed 10am–5pm,
Thurs 10am–9pm

- -

The MCA is the place to go to get your fill of interesting art – and it's the variety of work exhibited that makes the multi-level space so impressive. You could get lost in its colourful and quirky pockets for hours at a time, as you slowly make your way up to the rooftop cafe. If you want to take a piece of the experience home with you, the MCA shop is packed with a variety of toys, art, ornaments and books. The museum also hosts regular events that draw crowds in of an evening for talks, performances, music, drinks and more. Entry is free too, which is always a bonus.

THE ROCKS MARKETS

Playfair Street and Jack Mundey
Place, The Rocks
9240 8717
therocks.com
Foodie markets open
Fri 9am–3pm, regular markets
Sat–Sun 10am–5pm

The Rocks is already a quaint experience, but when its streets become lined with stallholders selling their creations, the charm goes up a level. With foodie markets taking place Fridays and the regular markets running on the weekend, this is a three-day treat for the senses. Things are slower and more relaxed here, and it creates a juxtaposition to the chaos of the CBD. Grab some Turkish gozleme and take your time exploring, munching and musing over the friendly atmosphere, and buying things like dresses, bags, jewellery, accessories and handmade crafts.

3.

KOBE JONES

29 Lime Street, King Street
Wharf, Sydney
9299 5290
kobejones.com.au
Open Mon–Fri 12–3pm,
Mon–Thurs 6pm–late,
Fri–Sun 5.30pm–late

Many venues have come and gone over the years in Darling Harbour, but Kobe Jones has remained. With a sumptuous bar area and divine dining room, it's the food that makes this Japanese restaurant a must-do. The philosophy is one of easy eating, with a menu that's perfect for sharing. You really can't visit without trying the Volcano Roll (oven-baked scallops, crab salad, special creams sauce and more). And you'd be mad not to try the parmesan motoyaki oysters. It's recommended you book ahead, and definitely ask for a seat on the balcony; there's no better way to dine than overlooking the harbour – with a cocktail in hand, of course!

4.

ANANAS

18 Argyle Street, The Rocks
9259 5668
ananas.com.au
Open Mon–Fri 12–3pm,
Mon–Thurs 6–10pm, Fri–Sat
5.30–11pm

Tucked away in the heart of The Rocks, Ananas is a Parisian feast for the senses. I'd even go so far as to say that it's the most decadent venue in Sydney. The decor inside is a little unusual but in the best way possible, giving a generous nod to the 1920s without feeling too themed. The dining space is large, sporting exposed brick walls, giant artworks, marble tabletops and gloriously golden pineapples to boot. The food is a bit of a French fantasy too (steak tartar, Burgundy snails or whole flounder) and if you throw in a bottle of bubbles you're set for a glam night.

5.

OPERA BAR

Lower concourse level Sydney
Opera House
9247 1666
operabar.com.au
Open Mon–Thurs 11.30am–
midnight, Fri 11.30am–1am,
Sat–Sun 9am–1am

There's no better place to
toast to your Sydney trip than
Opera Bar. It really has no
rival in the city, nestled under
the Sydney Opera House and
with such close proximity to
the water that you can almost
touch it. There's a range of
menus on offer, so while you'll
be tempted to sip and soak
up the sun in the alfresco
area, don't forget the food.
Breakfast on the weekends is
worth getting up early for (I'll
take the smashed avocado
with broadbean, mint and
dukkah) and the panoramic
views of the harbour –
especially as the sun sets –
might just deem you unable
to leave.

HOT TIP
A Friday evening, just
after 6pm, is the best time
to take in the post-work
party atmosphere.

THE GLENMORE HOTEL

96 Cumberland Street, The Rocks
9247 4794
theglenmore.com.au
Open Sun–Thurs 11am–
midnight, Fri–Sat 11am–1am

Claims like 'the best view in Sydney' get thrown around all the time, but Opera Bar aside, you really will be hard-pressed to find a better vantage point to take in such a sweeping view of the water than from the rooftop of The Glenmore Hotel. This iconic venue has been watching over the harbour since 1921, and its classic pub-style menu can't be beaten (try the fish and chips, which come out in a mini deep-fryer basket). You could explore the ground- and middle-floor levels, but when you're steps away from the Harbour Bridge and can see the Opera House from the rooftop, there's really only one place to be.

When local creative Kristy Withers isn't managing her children's decor and furniture store, Incy Interiors, she loves to get down by the water to take in the best venues Sydney has to offer. Here she dishes on the best-kept secrets in Sydney Harbour, Circular Quay and The Rocks.

How do you sum up the vibe of the Harbour?

I love that no matter what time of the night or day, this area is always buzzing. It's a hive of activity and there's something for everyone; be it a ferry ride for the family, a cocktail at The Shangri-La with the girls or a boys' night out at The Orient.

Best place to grab dinner by the water?

You cannot beat the Sydney institution, Café Sydney, for dinner. It combines the best view of the harbour, with Sydney's best seafood and an amazing wine list.

Must-do drinking destination?

You really cannot go past Opera Bar (*see* page 224) for a glass of wine in the sun. With direct views of the Harbour Bridge and all the action of the harbour, you can people-watch for hours. The Glenmore Hotel (*see* page 225) is another of my faves.

Any good spots that are family-friendly?

The area is jam-packed with activities for families. You can climb the iconic Harbour Bridge, take a tour of the solar system at The Observatory, attend the Baby Proms at The Opera House or take a bike ride around The Domain.

Where do you go to escape the city?

I go home! 2.5 years ago, we did a tree change and moved to a tiny little town in Central Western NSW, Millthorpe (just out of Orange). It has amazing cafes, restaurants and vineyards and only 600 residents, so it's where I go to recharge after a week spent working in the city.

ABOUT THE AUTHOR

Chris Carroll

I've lived in and around the city for over 10 years, but in true Sydneysider style, I never really ventured out to explore places outside of my hub. When I started my design blog – The Life Creative – over three years ago, it paved the way for me to start exploring the city more, uncovering a host of creativity along the way.

I called the many venues I visited 'decor destinations'; must-see bars, restaurants and cafes that had amazing fit-outs and furniture. I also carried out a series of store tours, to give readers a taste of what some of my fave homewares and stationery stores in Sydney had to offer.

Little did I know that all that shop sampling, cafe cruising and bar hopping would result in this book. And little did I know that the suburbs I had explored during my blogging adventures was just a small slice of one very big cake.

Sydney is like a million different cities in one. Turn down one street, wander down a laneway and you'll come out the other side in a suburb with an entirely different vibe. The multicultural aspect is one of the best things about this city, too, and you're always spoilt for choice in terms of the food and drink on offer.

I've explored many of the venues on my blog and in this book with my partner, Gavin, who helped me drink and eat my way through a lot of marvellous menus. I tend to like my venues more polished, while he prefers places with a little more grit. It makes for a really good balance and I hope you enjoy the diversity it's delivered when flicking through the pages of this book.

ACKNOWLEDGEMENTS

First of all, a big thank you to all of the restaurant owners, shop keepers, chefs, baristas and anyone else who I got to talk to during the process of putting this book together. Without a dedication to your own amazing venues, this book would have been impossible to produce.

I also have to thank some of the amazing PR people who got me into venues, supplied images, talked to owners on my behalf and secured some amazing interviews for me. You are the good guys and I really appreciate your efforts.

A big thanks to Lauren and Melissa at Hardie Grant for giving me the freedom to run with this book and for approaching me to begin with, and to Alice for her editorial encouragement.

Lastly, to Gavin – who listened to all of my first-world author problems – this book is partly yours, too. Thanks for consuming half of Sydney with me.

The publisher would like to acknowledge the following individuals and organisations:

Editorial manager
Melissa Kayser

Project manager
Lauren Whybrow

Editor
Alice Barker

Cartography
Emily Maffei, Bruce McGurty

Design
Michelle Mackintosh

Layout
Megan Ellis

Index
Max McMaster

Pre-press
Megan Ellis, Splitting Image

Photography credits

All photos © Chris Carroll, except for the following (letters indicate where multiple images appear on a page, from top to bottom, left to right):

i–ii Watsons Bay Boutique Hotel; iii–iv Flour and Stone; v–vi Dinosaur Designs; x–xi Opera Bar; 012–013 Styling and photography John Mangila; 014 Penny Farthing Design House; 015 The Essential Ingredient; 016 Belle Fleur; 017 The Cottage; 018: Wilhelmina's; 019 The Lodge; 024 b) Aquabumps; 025 b) Earth Food Store; 026 Da Orazio Pizza + Porchetta; 027 Shuk; 028–9 North Bondi Fish; 030–1 Icebergs; 032–3 The Eastern Hotel; 038 b) The Design Hunter; 039 b) The Design Hunter d) The Design Hunter f) The Design Hunter; 041: Bronte Road Bistro; 042 Three Blue Ducks; 052–3 Coogee Pavilion; 054 La Spiaggia; 055 Randwick Ritz Cinema; 062 a) Scanlan Theodore; 063 Dinosaur Designs; 064 Dale Whybrow; 065 Buffalo Dining Club; 066 Edition Coffee Roasters; 068 Four in Hand; 069 Love, Tilly Devine; 070–1 Print Room; 076 b) MJ Bale; 077 a) MJ Bale b) MJ Bale; 079 Laduree; 080 Char & Co; 081 Chiswick; 082 Indigo; 083 Sake; 091 Cornersmith; 094–5 Hartsyard; 100 Glebe Markets; 102 Booth Street Bistro; 104–5 The Royal Botanical; 106 b) The Little Guy; 107 b) The Little Guy; 112: Honey Bee Homewares; 114 Armchair Collective; 115: Papi Chulol 116–7 The Boathouse at Palm Beach; 118 Donny's Bar & Restaurant; 119 The Ivanhoe Hotel; 126–7 T Totaler; 138 a) Aija b) Papaya; 139 a) Papaya b) Aija c) Aija; 140 Bourke St Bakery; 142 The Oaks; 148 Becker Minty; 149 Flour and Stone; 150 Bottega Del Vino; 151 b) Gazebo; 152 b) Kingsleys Steak and Crabhouse, 153 b) Kingsleys Steak and Crabhouse; 154 b) Ms G's; 155 Peekaboos; 160 The Spa at the Darling; 161 Sydney Fish Market; 162 a) Adriano Zumbo b) Mamak; 163 a) Adriano Zumbo b) Mamak; 164 Flying Fish; 165 Lumi; 166–7 Sokyo; 176–7 White Rabbit Gallery; 184 Doyles on the Beach; 184 Jessica Knight; 186 a) Vaucluse House Tearooms b) Dunbar House; 187 Vaucluse House Tearooms b) Dunbar House c) Dunbar House; 188 a) Regatta Rose Bay; b) Watsons Bay Boutique Hotel; 189 a) Regatta Rose Bay; b) Watsons Bay Boutique Hotel; 196–7 Bills; 198–9 Gelato Messina; 200 b) The Beresford; 201 b) The Beresford; 208 Strand Arcade; 209 a) The Cornershop b) The Cornershop c) Strand Arcade; 210 a) The Tea Room b) Cheese & Wine Room; 211 a) The Tea Room b) Cheese & Wine Room; 212–3 Mr Wong's; 214 The Barbershop; 2015 Palmer & Co; 222 a) Kobe Jones b) Ananas; 223 a) Kobe Jones b) Ananas; 224 Opera Bar; 225 The Glenmore Hotel; 230–1 Lauren Whybrow; 232 The Boathouse at Palm Beach

Explore Australia Publishing Pty Ltd
Ground Floor, Building 1, 658 Church Street,
Richmond VIC 3121

Explore Australia Publishing Pty Ltd is a division of Hardie Grant Publishing Pty Ltd

hardie grant publishing

Published by Explore Australia Publishing Pty Ltd, 2016

A Cataloguing-in-Publication entry is available from the catalogue of the National Library of Australia at www.nla.gov.au

Maps imprint and currency © VAR Product and PSMA Data

"Copyright. Based on data provided under licence from PSMA Australia Limited (www.psma.com.au)".

Hydrography Data (May 2006)
Transport Data (May 2015)

Disclaimer
While every care is taken to ensure the accuracy of the data within this product, the owners of the data (including the state, territory and Commonwealth governments of Australia) do not make any representations or warranties about its accuracy, reliability, completeness or suitability for any particular purpose and, to the extent permitted by law, the owners of the data disclaim all responsibility and all liability (including without limitation, liability in negligence) for all expenses, losses, damages, (including indirect or consequential damages) and costs which might be incurred as a result of the data being inaccurate or incomplete in any way and for any reason.

ISBN-13 9781741174946

10 9 8 7 6 5 4 3 2 1

Printed and bound in China by 1010 Printing International Ltd

Publisher's disclaimer: The publisher cannot accept responsibility for any errors or omissions. The representation on the maps of any road or track is not necessarily evidence of public right of way. The publisher cannot be held responsible for any injury, loss or damage incurred during travel. It is vital to research any proposed trip thoroughly and seek the advice of relevant state and travel organisations before you leave. Every effort has been made to ensure that the information in this book is accurate at the time of going to press. The publisher welcomes information and suggestions for correction or improvement. Email: info@exploreaustralia.net.au

www.exploreaustralia.net.au

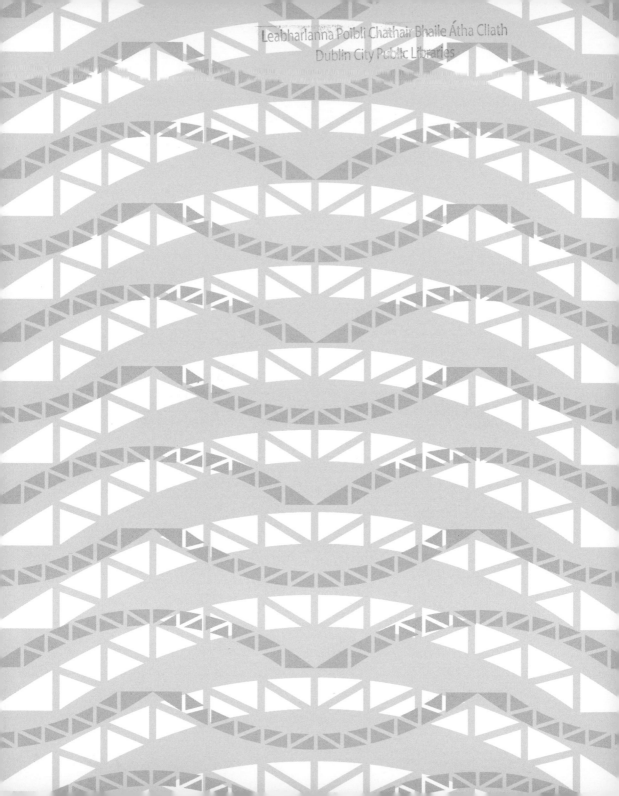